LEARN TO MAKE SOFT TOYS

Pamela Peake

GUILD PUBLISHING LONDON

Contents

1 Tools, Equipment and Materials

4 Basic Tools and Materials
6 Fabrics
6 Threads
7 Special techniques
7 Patterns and Cutting out
8 Seams and Stitches
10 Stuffing toys
12 Facial Features
13 Playing safe

2 Easy Soft Toys

14 Mouse
16 Mole
18 Woolly Hedgehog
21 Fur Hedgehog
22 Ladybird
24 Whale

3 Cuddly Animals

26 Teddy
30 Panda
32 Bear Cub
36 Fox
40 Rabbit
45 Variations on the patterns

4 Rag Dolls

46 Lara
50 Ziggy
56 Topsy-Turvy Sisters

5 Patchwork Toys

60 Alligator
62 Mice

This edition published 1987 by
Book Club Associates
by arrangement with
William Collins Sons & Co Ltd

Text and patterns © 1987 by Pamela Peake
Volume © 1987 by WI Books Ltd
39 Eccleston Street
London SW1W 9NT

Designed by Mike Leaman
Photographed by Tim Bishopp
Illustrated by Margaret Leaman
Series Editor Eve Harlow

Peake, Pamela
    Learn to make soft toys.—(Learn a craft)
    1. Soft toymaking
    I. Title   II. Series
    745.592'4   TT174.3

Typeset by Central Southern Typesetters, Eastbourne
Printed by New Interlitho, Italy

Introduction

Play is an essential function of childhood, and rag dolls, teddies and cuddly animals are just some of the many toys that children will play with during their formative years. Toys are the tools of play; they encourage the development of mental and physical skills, stimulate the imagination and help children to discover something about the world that they live in. In the broadest sense they both educate and amuse, but above all, toys, and especially dolls and cuddly animals, are fun.

To see the joy on a child's face when it is given an individually made toy is to understand why making soft toys has become such a popular craft. Functional as they may be, soft toys are also evocative of the treasured friends of one's own childhood and as such bring pleasure equally to maker and recipient.

The animals and dolls in this collection provide a structured course for beginners in making soft toys. They are made with straightforward cut, sew, turn and stuff techniques, so that no previous knowledge is required. All the patterns are full size and are accompanied by clear and detailed instructions, diagrams and photographs. Work your way through the collection systematically, starting with the very easy Mouse. Each following toy then introduces additional techniques, while the patterns build up in complexity. The experience gained by working in this way will provide you with an understanding of patterns, fabrics and all the basic skills necessary to make successful soft toys.

Tools, Equipment and Materials

Toymakers with some experience will be able to start wherever they like, making the toys in any sequence. Beginners however, are advised to exercise patience and to start by reading this chapter carefully and refer back as necessary. Most faults are caused by using the wrong materials or by working too quickly. This chapter will help to ensure that your toys will look like those in the pictures!

Most would-be toymakers are pleasantly surprised to discover that they already have all the tools and equipment necessary to make a start and do not have to make expensive purchases. Handstitching will even eliminate the need for a sewing machine. You will need the sewing aids that are usually used for dressmaking and in addition you will probably find some more useful tools in the workshop or garage. Most of the materials required are comparatively inexpensive.

Basic tools and materials

Scissors
Several pairs of scissors will be needed. First find an old pair of scissors for cutting out card patterns and paper. Dressmaking scissors with sharp cutting blades and pointed ends will be needed for cutting out cottons and other fabrics. Small embroidery scissors are useful for trimming the pile from fur or cutting felt away from fur when fur and felt have been topstitched together. They are also useful for clipping seams. Pinking shears help to cut decorative felt trims, but they are not essential.

Pliers
Choose pliers with long, thin points known as 'snipe-nosed' or 'electrician's' pliers. They are useful for pulling needles through bulky areas and for jointing toys. Wire snippers are used for cutting stiff wire when making a frame on which to wind wool for hair. They are also indispensable for removing wrongly-inserted safety eyes.

Stuffing tools
Most shapes can be stuffed by hand, using your fingers instead of stuffing sticks, but shapes like dolls' fingers require special tools to ensure that the filling reaches right down to the ends. A narrow stuffing stick can be made from dowelling. Shape the end, rather like a pencil tip, to make it easier to use. Some toymakers use pencils, knitting needles, chopsticks and even the points of scissors, all of which are useful aids providing that you take care not to puncture the fabric.

A pair of long forceps makes an ideal stuffing tool. Tiny wisps of stuffing can be caught in the forceps and wound around the tips. Insert the forceps into the cavity to be stuffed and hold them in place with the fingers of the left hand. Release the grip on the forceps and withdraw them carefully. Stuffing ball noses is very easy using forceps and the tips can also be used instead of an awl to make holes in fur fabric when inserting safety eyes.

Paper
Patterns are traced onto thin paper or tracing paper and then glued onto card to make card patterns.

Card
Card patterns are more durable than paper and provide a firm edge around which to draw. They are essential for cutting fur fabric because paper patterns tend to buckle on fur. Card patterns also eliminate the need for pins, which might get lost in the toy and prove dangerous. Card is also needed as a frame or former for winding wool when making hair and tails. Cereal packet card is quite adequate.

Keep card patterns together in an envelope or punch holes in them and slip them onto a length of twine.

Pencils
Pencils are used for marking patterns onto fabric. Use a 2B lead pencil on light-coloured furs and a white or yellow dressmaker's chalk on dark furs. Do not use felt-tipped pens as the ink can easily smudge on fur.

Red pencil is a useful alternative to lipstick for colouring cheeks. If facial features are drawn in the wrong place, a white plastic eraser will remove pencil marks from calico.

Pins
Try to keep the use of pins to a minimum to avoid a stray pin remaining in a toy and becoming a potential source of danger. Use pins with coloured heads so that you can keep count of them more easily.

Needles
Medium-sized sewing needles are used for hand-sewing seams while short, finer needles are needed for embroidering dolls' faces. Long darning needles are needed for shaping toys and for sewing on heads and limbs with strong thread. A bodkin is useful for threading elastic through puffs.

Glues
A thin coat of latex fabric adhesive will glue paper to card when making patterns and it will also stick felt to felt.

A clear, all-purpose glue which dries colourless yet remains flexible can be used to stick on small felt facial features.

Any unwanted smears of clear glue can be removed by sponging them with acetone; but beware – acetone is inflammable.

Additional aids

If you make a lot of soft toys it may be worthwhile to buy a fixing tool for inserting the eyes. A hammer, and a foam pad, as a cushion between the eye and table top will also be needed.

Last but not least, you will also need a steel-edged ruler, compasses, a craft knife, an awl or knitting needle for making holes and a punch for punching holes in felt.

Fabrics

Colour, texture and pattern contribute enormously to the appeal and success of a toy. In some instances colour and pattern actually identify the animals. Black and white are as essential for the panda as red and black are for the seven-spot ladybird and while the fox is recognisable from the design, realistic colours certainly enhance his character.

Other animals can be made in colours of your choice since they are already easily recognisable by their design. The soft, cuddly fur animals are equally attractive whether they are made in pastel colours for the very young or in the more realistic colours preferred by older children. The choice is yours, but you should take into account the age of the child who is to receive the toy.

Other fabric properties must also be considered. Some fabrics are closely woven and will stuff firmly while other stretchy fabrics will need different treatment. Fabrics which fray easily will prove difficult for beginners but this does not necessarily mean that they should not be used. Washability is important, especially when making toys for the very young.

Fur fabrics

Fur fabric is very popular with toymakers because it comes in such a variety of pile depths and colours, enabling a wide range of animals to be made. Pile can be short, medium or long, with wonderfully soft textures. Plain colours are plentiful and there are also patterns to choose from, some of them so realistic that toys made with them seem very life-like. Most of the animals in this book have been made from short pile fur, not only

because it is easier to work with, but because it is most suitable for young children. Long pile can become matted and unhygienic when chewed, or cause breathing problems if a child sleeps with the toy near its face.

All the patterns in this book state the type of fur needed to make a particular toy and you should try to find the type recommended when choosing fur. Shiny furs are called 'polished' and matt furs are 'unpolished'.

When buying fur, run your fingers over the pile to test its quality. If the pile parts easily and you can see the backing from the right side, it is of a poor quality. Ideally, a dense pile is required and this will cost slightly more.

Felt

The very first commercially produced soft toys were made of felt and this fabric has remained a firm favourite with toymakers ever since. A wide range of colours is available in small squares, so felt is frequently recommended to contrast with fur for lining ears, and making soles, paws, beaks and eyes.

Felt varies in thickness (something which should be checked when buying, as thin felt will stretch and split when stuffed). Hold felt up to the light to find the thin spots. Sometimes an iron-on, non-woven backing will strengthen a weak felt.

Felt does not wash well so another fabric should be substituted when washability is important.

Fleece

Fleece is used to make children's dressing gowns and because of its softness and washability it is a useful substitute for felt when lining ears and making the soles of paws and feet. Fleece may be woven or knitted and the pile is part of the backing. It is not really suitable for making the skin of toys except for very small, simple 'clutch' characters, because it stretches and distorts when stuffed.

Velour

Modern velour may be a pile or nap fabric. A nap fabric is one which has to be cut in one direction only. Velour can be made from cotton, wool or a mixture of fibres. Again, it is a useful substitute for felt when a washable contrast is needed. Dress velour tends to be washable,

whereas furnishing velour often needs dry cleaning so check before buying.

Calico

Calico, a traditional doll-making fabric, has been used to make the dolls in this book.

Calico is a closely woven fabric and toys made from it can be stuffed firmly. Choose a substantial, opaque calico. Remove the dressing by washing the fabric, then pull into shape and iron dry while it is slightly damp. Calico can be coloured to make darker skins by soaking it in an infusion of tea bags in water with a little vinegar added.

Stockinette

Stockinette is a knitted stretch fabric which can be used for making toys with rounded cheeks and chubby fingers. This is achieved by needle-modelling or shaping with a needle.

Cotton and cotton lawn

Dolls' clothes are made from dress-weight cottons and fine cotton lawn. For small dolls particularly, select fabrics with patterns of the correct scale.

Interfacing

Soft, iron-on, non-woven interfacing will give body to thin felt and will control the amount of stretch when used as a backing for stockinette. Firm iron-on, non-woven interfacing is a good weight on which to embroider animal eyes. There is also an iron-on stretchy, non-woven interfacing. This stretches on the width or on the bias, but not on the length so it is also useful for backing stockinette. Dolls will stuff and shape depending on the quality of interfacing used. It is advisable to test interfacing first before proceeding with a project.

Follow the manufacturer's instructions when using iron-on interfacings for backing fabrics.

Threads

Sewing threads for seams should match the fabric. Use synthetic threads for man-made fabrics such as furs, and cotton thread for natural fabrics. Alternatively, use an all-purpose thread which can be used for both types of fabric. All-purpose threads are cotton-covered polyester threads that combine strength with sheen and are suitable for both heavy and lightweight fabrics as well as stretch

knits without snapping. These threads can be ironed at high temperatures, do not knot or tangle during hand-sewing, and come in many shades.

A much stronger thread is needed for closing seams and sewing heads, limbs and ears to bodies. Several different threads are suitable, ranging from button thread to crochet cotton and linen upholstery threads. Test threads before using them on a toy to make sure that they are really strong and that you cannot break them easily. Choose a neutral colour to work with.

Six-stranded embroidery cotton is used to embroider features. Animal noses are usually worked with six strands, while dolls' eyelashes may only need two or three strands.

Nylon sewing thread is suitable for soft whiskers. It is available from furnishing departments of large stores.

Special Techniques
Patterns

All the patterns in this book are full size and ready for immediate use once they have been transferred to card. Trace the master pattern off the page on tracing paper and then glue it to card. Transfer all letters, instructions, arrows and lines from the original pattern.

When the glue is completely dry, cut

out on the pencil line. A slightly larger pattern will be obtained by cutting outside the pencil line. On head pattern pieces, pierce a hole through the card to mark the position of the eye.

Some pattern pieces are shown as one half only, with a 'place on fold' direction. To make a complete pattern, lay the folded edge of a piece of tracing paper against the fold line of the master pattern and trace off the outline with HB pencil. Turn the tracing over and re-trace the outline to obtain a complete pattern.

Pattern pieces with almost similar outlines are drawn together as if they were one. Examples are the Front and Back bodies of the Dolls (see page 50) and the Front and Back Bodice and Pants (page 52). Take care to draw the shared outline first, then the relevant different part or parts.

The Mouse, Hedgehogs, Mole, Ladybird and Whale share several pattern pieces but they are not necessarily used in the same way. For example, the pile of the fur on the base of the Whale runs in the opposite direction to that of the other animals. To avoid confusion, make a completely separate set of pattern pieces for each animal. The parts needed are listed under 'Making the pattern' in the relevant instructions. Transfer only those markings needed for the animal being made.

For circular patterns, measurements are given for the diameter of the circle. Circles can be drawn directly onto card

with compasses set to the radius of the circle (half the diameter).

Measurements for other regular shapes, such as squares and rectangles for skirts, frills, tails and bias strips are also given in the instructions, and these may be drawn directly onto the wrong side of the fabric. Paper or card patterns can be made if the toy is being made more than once.

Pattern markings

Each pattern piece is identified by the name of the animal or doll and by the name of the relevant part of the body or clothing. The number of pieces to be cut is also given. Letters on the patterns relate to the step-by-step instructions.

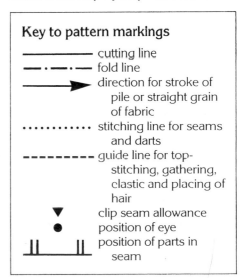

Key to pattern markings

——————— cutting line

—·—·—·— fold line

————▶ direction for stroke of pile or straight grain of fabric

············ stitching line for seams and darts

- - - - - - - guide line for top-stitching, gathering, elastic and placing of hair

▼ clip seam allowance

● position of eye

‖   ‖ position of parts in seam

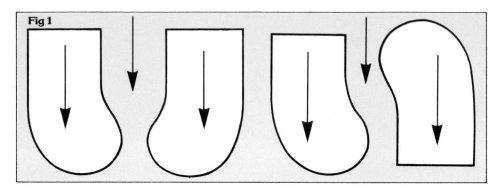

Pattern layout

Before positioning pattern pieces on fur fabric check the direction in which the pile lies. Lay the fur on the table with the pile side facing upwards. Run the flat of your hand along the pile. In one direction the fur will be raised and ruffled, while in the other direction it will lie flat and feel very smooth. Fold the fur over and draw an arrow in pencil on the back, pointing in the same direction as the smooth stroke of the pile. Turn the fur over and lay it, pile side to the table.

When laying pattern pieces, position the largest pieces and long gussets first. Smaller pieces can then be fitted in more economically.

'Cut two' on the pattern means two pieces cut the same way. 'Cut a pair' means cut one piece, then turn the pattern over and cut the second piece, so that you have a right and left side. Do not turn the pattern piece upside down.

Fig 1 illustrates this; the Arm piece layout on the left is correct with both directional arrows laid the same way while the layout on the right is incorrect.

Read through the instructions to make sure that all the pattern pieces are positioned and sufficient fabric has been allowed for pieces which may be given by measurement only.

When you are satisfied with the layout, make a plan of it for future reference. Draw round all the card pieces, using a soft, dark pencil on light-coloured furs and a soft, light-coloured chalk on dark furs. Mark round the card pieces in the same way when working on cottons. A 6mm (¼in) seam allowance is included on all pattern pieces, except those which are used to cut out felt, so the cutting line will be just inside the pencil line.

Cutting out

When cutting fur fabric, slide the point of the lower blade of the scissors beneath the fur and up against the backing to

Fig 1 *The Arms layout left is correct for cutting a pair. The pile strokes downwards on both pieces so that when they are stitched together the fur on the outside runs the same way. The layout on the right is incorrect because the pile will stroke the wrong way on one side when the Arms are stitched together*

avoid damaging the pile. Once the pattern has been cut, gently pull the fabric apart so as not to disturb pile along the cut edge. Never try to save time by cutting fur in double thickness.

Pattern pieces to be cut from cotton fabrics should be positioned with their straight grain arrows lying parallel to the selvedge. As felt is a non-woven fabric, patterns for felt pieces have no arrows. However, when cutting similar pieces align them in the same direction so that they stretch the same way.

Seams and stitches

A seam allowance of 6mm (¼in) is included on all pattern pieces except on those that are cut from felt. These generally have a 3mm (⅛in) seam allowance. Extra fabric is allowed for hems and for gathering the waists of skirts.

For all the toys, seams may be stitched by machine or sewn by hand using Backstitch (Fig 2). Choose whichever method suits you although some intricate parts are more easily sewn by hand.

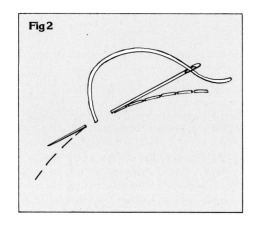

Fig 2 *Backstitch is used for starting and finishing lines of stitching and for sewing strong seams by hand. To work the stitch, and working from right to left, bring the thread through and insert it one stitch back, bringing the needle out one stitch ahead of the stitch just made*

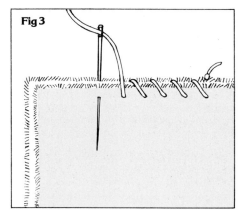

Fig 3 *Oversew edges of fur fabric starting 12mm (½ in) from the end to allow for crossing seams without bulk*

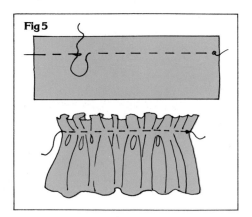

Fig 5 *Work running stitches along the edge to be gathered. Pull up the thread to bring the fabric to the desired width*

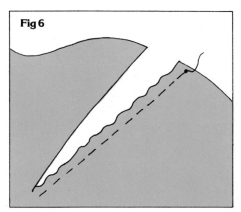

Fig 6 *Easing the fullness of one long edge to a shorter edge by gathering the long edge*

Seaming fur fabric Seaming fur fabric toys is quite different from seaming dolls or dresses. The two pieces to be joined are first oversewn together to prevent the fur slipping when it is stitched. Place the edges together tucking in the pile and start the oversewing approximately 12mm (½in) from the end (Fig 3). This is done so that crossing seams can be opened out to lie flat.

After oversewing, complete the seam with machine-stitching or by hand using Backstitch. When hand sewing, take small, firm stitches. Check finished seams for any weak areas and clean seams by releasing trapped pile. This is done by using a teasel brush or by flicking a needle over the seam, easing out the pile.

Hand-sewn fur fabric toys generally feel much softer than those that have been machine-stitched.

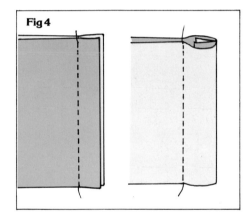

Fig 4 *French seam: with wrong sides of fabric facing, stitch half the seam allowance from the edge. Trim the seam allowance. Turn fabric right sides facing and stitch on the seam line, enclosing raw edges*

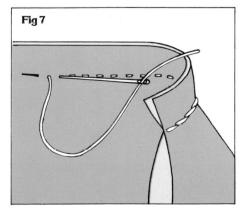

Fig 7 *Stab stitch is worked in a similar way to Backstitch but the stitches are smaller*

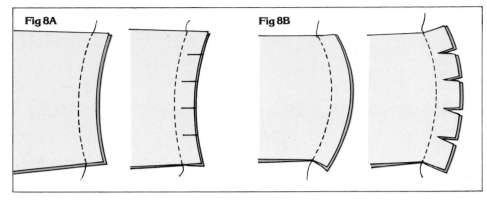

Fig 8A *Stitch along the seam line, slash into the allowance up to the seam on an inward curve*

Fig 8B *Stitch along the seam line, cut notches into the allowance to reduce bulk on an outward curve*

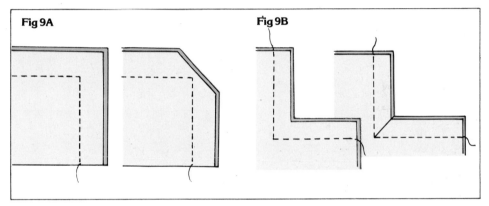

Fig 9A *Stitch the corner then trim away the seam allowance diagonally to reduce bulk*

Fig 9B *Stitch an inner corner, slash into the angle to the stitching to release tension*

Seaming cotton fabric Cotton fabrics can be seamed either by machine or by hand using Backstitch. Hold pieces together with basting stitches worked on the seam line before seaming. Always remove basting threads after stitching.

As dolls are stuffed very firmly seams need to be very secure. This is achieved by working a second row of stitching at stress points or by stitching over an entire seam. Hand-sewn seams are usually strong enough if double thread is used and corners are reinforced.

French seams are used on some of the dolls' clothing. These are strong seams which give a finished look to the wrong side of the fabric and prevent fraying. Fig 4 shows how a French seam is worked.

Gathering When one piece of fabric is longer than the piece to which it is being joined, it will have to be eased or gathered to fit. An example of this is when a skirt is gathered at the waist to fit the bodice (Fig 5), or less usually, when unequal-sided darts or head pieces have to be fitted together. To ease, make a row of long running stitches on the longer piece of fabric. Pull up on the thread and spread the fullness along the seam line to the required length (Fig 6).

Topstitching When small pieces are put together (such as the ears of hedgehogs and mice) they are topstitched together. Wrong sides are placed together and the piece does not need turning. Top-stitching can be done by machine-stitching or by hand, using Backstitch (Fig 2) or Stab stitch (Fig 7).

Trimming seams In certain circumstances, seam allowances need trimming if they are not to pucker and form wrinkles and lumps. This usually happens at curves and corners.

Fig 8a shows how to trim an outward curve to reduce bulk, while Fig 8b shows how to trim an inward curve and clip it to release tension. For fur fabric animals, this may mean cutting into the oversewing, but this does not matter since the oversewing is only a form of basting.

Corners are cut away to reduce bulk (Fig 9a). Clip into inward corners to release tension on the fabric and to prevent wrinkles on the right side (Fig 9b).

Stitches

Ladder stitch

All toy skins have a seam opening through which they are turned right side out and stuffed. This opening along the seam line is closed with Ladder stitch worked with a strong thread (Fig 1). Legs, arms, ears and heads can also be sewn to the body with this stitch. Limbs that have a tendency to splay out can be corrected with Ladder stitch.

Decorative stitches

Decorative stitches are used to embroider the facial features and to work details such as claws. Stem stitch, Straight stitch and Satin stitch are the only stitches you need to know in order to decorate the toys in the book.

Fillings

Fillings for toymaking can range from lumpy foam chips to fine, resilient polyester fibres, from dense sawdust to polystyrene granules or from heavy, cut-up waste fabrics to non-resilient kapok. The choice of filling is very important because it influences the shape, weight and texture of a toy.

Polyester fibre filling has been used for all the toys in this book, as it conforms to established health and safety standards. Polyester fibre is a very resilient filling which springs back to shape after crushing. It handles easily, is flameproof, clean, weighs little and washes well, drying quickly because it is non-absorbent. Polyester fibre is also white, which makes it an ideal stuffing for both dolls and pastel-coloured fur toys.

Stuffing toys

The filling should never be used straight from the bag. Always tease the fibres apart first to fluff them up and increase the bulk. This teasing will, at the same time, locate any lumps or foreign bodies, which can then be removed.

Sometimes a pattern provides two openings to make stuffing easier. For instance, the Rabbit on page 40 has an additional opening at the back between the legs. Having stuffed the body from the feet upwards it may be necessary to add more filling to the feet to make the rabbit stand securely, but do not overstuff as this will spread the feet, alter the centre of gravity and cause the toy to fall forward.

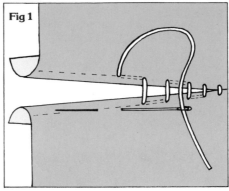

Some of the dolls' heads can be stuffed from both the neck and the crown to ensure a firm fill with rounded cheeks.

As you stuff, turn the toy so that it is evenly filled. Roll and stroke the limbs

Fig 1 *Ladder stitch: work from right to left with doubled thread. Slide the needle along the back of the fabric on the seam line for 6mm ($\frac{1}{4}$ in) then bring it through to the front and insert it in the seam on the opposite side of the opening. Continue, working a few stitches, then pull up the thread. Stitches should be almost invisible*

between the fingers to make sure that no lumps form. Lumps cannot be disguised or stuffed away but must be removed and filling teased apart and then re-inserted. Close openings with Ladder stitch (refer to Fig 1), inserting more stuffing behind the newly-formed seam.

Although the same filling has been used for all the toys in this book, it has not always been used in the same way. Some toys are stuffed gently so that they are lightweight and soft rather than rock hard; others must be firm all over while several are gently stuffed in some parts and firmly stuffed in others.

The Mouse, Hedgehogs, Mole, Ladybird, Whale and Bear cub are really just stuffed bags with no awkward corners.

Take care to stuff firm snouts and don't overstuff the top of the limbs or they will splay. The Fox also needs a firm snout and careful stuffing at the top of the front legs. The Teddy and Panda have firmly stuffed bodies, heads and lower limbs, but the upper limbs are loosely stuffed to make them flexible,

enabling the toys to sit more easily.

The calico dolls are similar to the Bears, with limbs made flexible by less filling in the appropriate places. Dolls have smaller necks than animals, which can present problems. In this book you will find that the dolls have been given necks which are stuffed firmly and inserted into the head, a method which does away with the need for support rods.

Because knitted fabric has a tendency to stretch easily, stockinette dolls should not be over-filled.

Facial Features

The character of toys is largely determined by the choice and positioning of facial features. Happiness, for instance, is conveyed by a smiling mouth, while youthfulness can be indicated by positioning the eyes slightly lower down and further apart on the face. This is easier to do on dolls than on animals, although larger eyes can often indicate youthfulness in an animal. Features expressing emotion are very important to the appeal of a toy.

Several different methods have been used to make the faces of the toys in this book. The majority of the animals have manufactured safety eyes with embroidered or stuffed fabric ball noses. Dolls have embroidered or felt features with softly-coloured cheeks.

Eyes

Commercially-made eyes range in size from 6mm to 24mm (¼–1in) and there are several colours to choose from. Cats' eyes with characteristic slit pupils are also available. All safety eyes have a shank which is pushed through a small hole in the fabric skin and fixed in place with a metal or plastic washer (Fig 1).

Patterns are marked with the fixing position of safety eyes and a hole should be made in the card pattern on this spot so that the position can be marked on the wrong side of the fur fabric with pencil. Do not make a hole in the fur

fabric at this stage because the position needs checking on the finished skin. If a narrower or wider seam allowance has been taken in making up this could affect the positions of the eyes. Work a tailor's tack over the pencil marks so that the eye positions can be seen on the right side of fabric.

Insert the stuffing into the head and then hold the eyes against the marking threads. If you are happy with the colour, size and position of the eyes, remove the stuffing and make a small hole with an awl or knitting needle on the marked spot.

Some knitted furs stretch and thus a small eye hole could expand, thus making it easier for the eye to be pulled out by little fingers. There are several ways of strengthening a hole to prevent this eventuality. Cut a small felt patch approximately 2.5cm (1in) in diameter and punch a hole in the middle of it. Spread glue on one side of the patch, align it with the eye holes on the wrong side of fabric and then press the patch firmly into place. Alternatively, iron a patch of non-woven interfacing over the eye area as the relevant pattern piece is cut out.

Noses

Commercially-made safety noses are either black and designed for animals such as dogs, bears, and seals or they are red balls, which are more suitable for clowns. Noses are fixed with a washer in the same way as eyes. Some nose

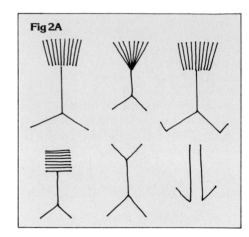

Fig 2A *Nose and mouth shapes for animals including Bears and Rabbits: the last shape represents a rodent's incisor teeth*

shanks have a hole through them, which enables the nose to be stitched in place. In this case, strong thread is tied onto the shank and is then threaded into a long darning needle. Finish the thread end by Backstitching along the neck around the seam line. In this book, only the Fox has a safety nose. All the other animals have either embroidered noses or stuffed fabric ball noses.

Embroidered features

Embroidered features have been used for the dolls in this book and they are ideal for any toy made for very young children. Embroidered features are completely safe, washable and unique, as no two toymakers ever work in quite the same way.

Fitting safety eyes

Safety eyes are supplied with washers (Fig 1a). Plastic washers fit on ridged shanks and as the washer is pushed onto the shank it passes over each ridge until it lodges behind the eye, trapping the fur fabric between eye and washer.

Metal washers are made in two different styles and are fixed in different ways. Flat-edged washers can be fixed with finger pressure alone (Fig 1b), while lipped-edged washers need a special fixing tool and have to be hammered in place (Fig 1c).

The diagrams show how the eye is fixed in place with the washer locked against the shank. The teeth on the washer bite against the shank as it is pushed down firmly, keeping the washer level all the time. If the washer gets stuck at an angle and it cannot be moved in either direction, it may have to be cut off with wire snippers, which is tricky, but not

impossible. Cut across two of the narrow parts and the washer should lift off. The washer cannot be used again.

An eye that has been inserted in the wrong place can be removed in the same way. Darn the hole neatly from the wrong side afterwards and it will be possible to insert another safety eye. Otherwise embroider an eye to cover the darn.

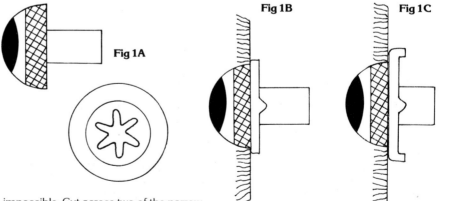

Fig 1A *Cross section of a safety eye with a shank and a flat view of a washer*

Fig 1B *A safety eye fixed in place with fur between the eye and the washer. This is a flat-edged washer, fixed with finger pressure*

Fig 1C *A safety eye fixed in place with a lipped-edge washer that requires a special tool for assembly*

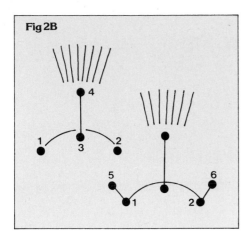

Fig 2B

Fig 2B *Embroidering a mouth: work Satin stitches for the nose, then bring the needle out at 1 and insert it at 2, leaving a long loose stitch on the surface. Bring the needle out at 3 and, catching the long surface stitch 1–2, pull up the thread. Finish the mouth by inserting the needle at 4. A happy mouth can be worked by adding Straight stitches from 5–1 and 6–2*

Noses Animal noses are usually made as a block of Satin stitches worked in brown, black or a neutral coloured stranded embroidery cotton. Fig 2a shows a selection of nose shapes together with mouths, which are worked at the same time. Use three or six strands of embroidery thread and begin by anchoring the thread in the neck seam, out of sight, then outline the nose before filling it in with Satin stitch. Fig 2b shows the sequence for making the mouth.

After working the mouth (see 1–2), the thread is caught down with tiny stitches which disappear into the pile (3–4, 1–5, 2–6). Pull slightly on the thread as you cut the end so that it slips back into the head.

Embroidered eyes These are suitable for any of the fur toys and are an acceptable alternative if there is concern about using other types of eye. Embroider both eyes at the same work session so that they are more likely to match.

Figs 3a–3d shows how to work embroidered eyes.

Faces Dolls' faces are embroidered directly onto the finished, stuffed heads, a method of working which ensures that the features will be correctly positioned on the taut fabric.

The face can be drawn directly onto the fabric with a sharp, soft pencil and any wrongly placed or unwanted lines can be removed with a white plastic eraser. (Test the pencil and the efficiency of the eraser by drawing on the top of the head first.) You may prefer to trace the

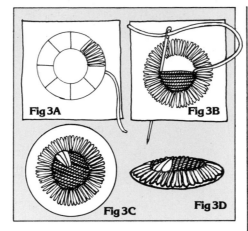

Fig 3A   Fig 3B   Fig 3C   Fig 3D

Fig 3A *Draw a circle for the eye iris, then a smaller circle for the pupil on non-woven interfacing. Section the pupil with Straight stitches. Embroider the iris with Satin stitches*

Fig 3B *Work the pupil in Satin stitch using black stranded embroidery cotton, setting the stitches horizontally*

Fig 3C *Work a highlight with a few white Straight stitches at top right. Cut out the eye shape 6mm (¼ in) from the edge of the eye*

Fig 3D *Run a gathering thread round the edges and pull up the stitches. Flatten the eye in the fingers and sew to the toy with hemming stitches*

face onto tracing paper and then transfer the features to the fabric using dressmaker's carbon paper.

Pass the needle into the head from behind the ear and bring it out at the place intended to begin embroidery. Use a fine, sharp needle to avoid making large holes in the fabric and embroider features with one, two or three strands of embroidery cotton. Keep features simple until confidence is gained.

Cheeks can be blushed lightly with powder, lipstick or coloured pencil as desired.

Fabric features

Eyes are easily made from felt, quickly cut out and sewn together, then hemmed or glued in place. Felt eyes are best sewn to the face and used only on toys that aren't going to need much washing. A smearing of clear adhesive on the back of a felt square enables clean circles to be cut and also strengthens the felt. Felt and satin have been used in this book to make ball noses. For a realistic effect nostrils can be indicated by two single Detached Chain stitches.

Playing safe

Playtime should be a happy, relaxed experience, free from the worry that childrens' toys could be a potential danger. Although in the past, children were often injured by unsafe toys, strict safety laws and the constant education of the public have remedied this unhappy state of affairs.

A good, safe toy should relate to the age, development and nature of the child who will be using it, as what is safe for one child may not necessarily be suitable for another.

Remember, too, that children often have younger brothers and sisters. Check that the toys are being played with by the children for whom they were intended and in the manner for which they were designed, for mishaps are more likely to happen when toys are in the wrong hands. You should check from time to time that soft toys, like all other toys, are clean and in good repair.

Safety features and any other hard fixtures on a soft toy must be securely embedded so that children can neither pull them out nor bite them off. Embroidered eyes and felt cut-out shapes are alternatives to safety features. Use these in preference to safety features when making toys for very young children because they tend to put toys to their mouths.

If a ribbon is required around a neck, stitch it securely to the body. Avoid using any trims with sharp points on clothing and shoes.

Fabrics should be colourfast, so that dyes do not react to saliva or sweat. Pile fabrics should be flame-retardant.

Adhesives used to bond fabrics together should be compatible with cleaning requirements for those fabrics.

Providing these guidelines are followed and the animals and dolls made as directed, there should be no problems.

Easy Soft Toys

A very simple yet effective soft toy can be made by using a three-piece pattern consisting of paired sides and base. The addition of ears, tail, limbs or spots, together with careful selection of fabrics and colour provides many variations to the basic pattern. Use the pattern to become familiar with a variety of techniques before moving on to make the animals in Chapter Three.

Mouse

The Mouse has a stuffed ball-nose and a velvet tubing tail. This simple, attractive toy makes a good first project for a beginner.

Materials required

Finished size 17cm (7in)-long body, 38cm (15in) to the tip of the tail
23cm *(9in)* of 46cm *(18in)*-wide short pile fur
24cm *(9½in)* of velvet tube for tail
1 pair of 15mm *(⅝in)*-diameter amber safety eyes
50g *(2oz)* of stuffing
Small piece of fleece for ear linings
Small piece of shiny pink fabric for nose
Clear all-purpose glue in a tube

Making the pattern

From the trace-off pattern Fig 1 on page 17 trace the Mouse's Side Body, Base, Mouse Nose and Mouse Ear Outer and Lining.

Make a set of card patterns following the technique described on page 7. Transfer relevant markings. A seam allowance of 6mm *(¼in)* is included on all pieces.

Cutting out

Cut out a pair of Side Bodies from fur fabric with the pile stroking down the body from top to base (see pile direction arrow on the pattern Fig 1). Cut one Base from fur fabric, following the direction arrow. Cut one Nose from pink fabric. Cut a pair of Outer Ears from fur fabric and a pair of Ear Linings from fleece.

To make the Mouse

Stitch the darts on each Side Body and finger-press the seams open. With right sides together, stitch the Side Bodies together along the centre back seam from A to B. Stitch under the snout C–D (A–C remains open). Position the Base and stitch the Side Bodies to the Base D–E. Leave the seam E–B–E open. Turn the skin right side out.

Insert the nozzle of a glue tube into one end of the velvet tubing and gently squeeze out a little glue. Wait until the glue becomes tacky before pressing the sides of the tube together and moulding a tip to the tail. Place the open end of the tail against the seam at B and with raw edges level, hand-sew the tail in place on the right side of the body (Fig 1 this page).

Eyes Check the eye positions. Insert the safety eyes when you are satisfied that they are in the right position (refer to Figs 1a, b and c on page 12).

Stuff the body firmly, working from the nose to the tail. Close the open seam E–B–E using Ladder stitch (see Fig 1, page 10). Clean all seams by releasing any trapped fur (see page 9).

Nose Run a gathering thread around the pink nose circle about 6mm *(¼in)* in from the edge. Pull up the thread, inserting a piece of stuffing, and continue pulling up the gathering thread, drawing all the raw edges together into a stalk (see Fig 2). Fasten off the thread end securely. Hold the mouse in the palm of the left hand and encircle the snout with thumb and fingers. Use the end of a pencil to push the raw edge of the snout, A–C, inside the head. Push the gathered 'stalk' of the nose through the opening. Ladder-stitch in place.

By having an open snout it is possible

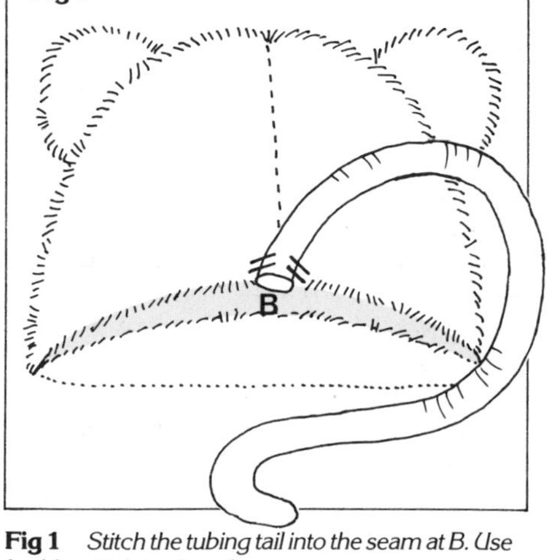

Fig 1   *Stitch the tubing tail into the seam at B. Use Ladder stitch to close the seam*

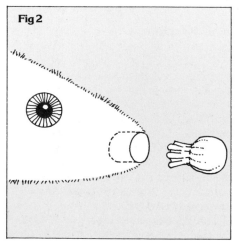

Fig 2   *Insert the 'stalk' of the fabric-covered ball nose into the snout cavity at A-C. Ladder-stitch*

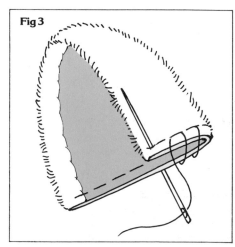

Fig 3   *Fold over one-third of the Ear and then oversew the edge to hold the fold in place*

to lengthen or shorten the head for different animals. It also provides a satisfactory method for sewing on ball noses.

Making the Ears
Run a gathering thread around the curved edge of an Outer Ear piece. Pull up on the thread until the curve matches the curve of the Ear Lining. Sew both Ear pieces together by hand wrong sides

facing, using Backstitch; this will keep the gathers evenly distributed and stop pleats forming. Turn the completed Ear right side out and check that the Ear rolls onto the lining (see Fig 3). Re-sew if it does not roll. Clean the seam and baste the raw edges together.

Fold over approximately one-third of the Ear onto the lining. Oversew the raw edges to hold the fold in place, Fig 3. Make a second Ear in the same way.

Position the Ears on the Head above and behind the Eyes, with folded edges about 6mm (1/4in) away from the centre back seam. Set them slightly slanted outwards. Ladder-stitch the front side of the Ears to the head first, taking stitches through the lining about 6mm (1/4in) up from the raw edge. Then work around to the back, taking stitches through the fur only. The base of the Ear will be hidden, as the lining and fur are spread apart.

Woolly Hedgehog

The Hedgehog is yet another adaptation of the basic pattern and the prickles are made from knitting yarn, stitched into fringes and then sewn to the body in rows.

Materials required

Finished size 19cm (7½in) long
23cm (9in) by 46cm (18in)-wide tweed
   or wool fabric
50g (2oz) stuffing
Small piece of felt for nose
Small piece of non-woven interfacing for
   eyes
1 skein stranded embroidery cotton,
   Black
50g (2oz) of mohair knitting yarn
28g (1oz) of double knitting yarn
Matching button thread

Making the pattern

From the trace-off pattern Fig 1 on page 17 trace the Woolly Hedgehog's Side Body and Base. Trace the smaller, Hedgehog's Nose. Make a set of card patterns and transfer relevant markings. A seam allowance of 6mm (¼in) is included on all pattern pieces.

Cutting out

Using the card patterns, cut a pair of Side Bodies and a Base from fabric and a Nose from felt.

To make the Hedgehog

Assemble the Side Body and Base following the instructions given for the Mouse on page 14. Turn the skin to the right side. Stuff the toy. Make a felt ball Nose and sew it in place, following the instructions given for the Mouse.
Eyes Embroider 18mm (¾in)-diameter eyes on non-woven interfacing. Finish the eyes as directed in Figs 3a–3d, page 13. Sew the eyes in place on the Hedgehog at the position shown on the pattern for the Mole eyes.

Making the prickles

Woolly prickles for Hedgehogs may be made from any thickness of wool and in a variety of colours and lengths to suit the toy. The quantities given in the materials list are more than sufficient to make one hedgehog. The wool and mohair yarn are used mixed together.

Cut the yarn into seventy-two 91cm (36in) lengths. Lay twenty-four strands side by side and machine-stitch across the strands starting 4cm (1½in) from one end and then at 7.5cm (3in) intervals. The last seam is 4cm (1½in) from the far end. Cut midway between the lines of stitching to make twelve small pieces of fringing. (Fig 1.)

Place six of these small pieces in line with each other matching the rows of stitching (see Fig 1). Machine-stitch the pieces together working over the original stitching line to make a continuous strip. Repeat with the remaining six pieces of fringing.

Take another twenty-four strands of yarn and sew them in the same way to make another twelve pieces of fringing. This time make two strips of five and seven pieces respectively. Repeat with the remaining twenty-four strands of yarn. This should result in six strips, two composed of six pieces of fringing, two of five pieces and two of seven pieces.
Attaching the prickles Lay a five-piece strip over the Hedgehog just behind the eyes so that it frames the face. Backstitch in place with button thread, taking stitches through the central seam.

Position a six-strip length behind the first strip and Backstitch in place. (The prickles will stand up as each strip is added.) Continue working towards the rear of the toy as shown in Fig 2.

When the body is evenly covered, brush the prickles so that they stand up, then carefully trim any ends that are too long. Trim the prickles around the lower edge of the face to give a pleasing finish (see picture).

Fig 1 *Stitch across the lengths of yarn then cut between the rows of stitching. Lay the fringes together edge to edge and machine-stitch over the previous stitching line to make a long strip*

Fig 2 *Sew strips of fringing to the Hedgehog body in the indicated order*

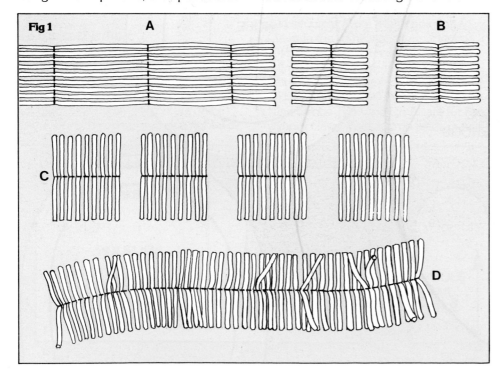

Fig 1

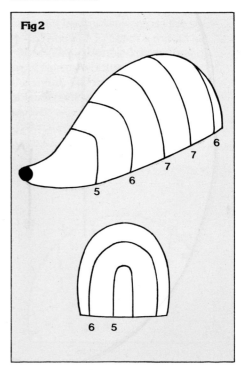

Fig 2

Fur Hedgehog

This toy makes use of a special fur resembling hedgehog prickles. The head is made in a contrasting fur fabric.

Materials required

Finished size 17cm (7in) long
23cm (9in)-square of hedgehog fur
23cm (9in)-square of short pile fur
50g (2oz) of stuffing
1 pair of 12mm (½in)-diameter amber safety eyes
Small piece of brown felt for ears
Small piece of shiny black fabric for nose

Making the pattern

From the trace-off pattern Fig 1 on page 17 trace the Fur Hedgehog's Nose, Base and Side Body, taking note of the pile direction arrows, and the special cutting line for this pattern at the 'neck'. From trace-off pattern Fig 1 this page, trace the Hedgehog's Head and Ear. Make card patterns. Transfer all markings. A seam allowance of 6mm (¼in) is included on all fur pieces. No seam allowance is included on the Ear.

Cutting out

From the special Hedgehog fur, cut a pair of Side Bodies with the fur stroking forwards towards the face, so that the prickles stand up when the animal is stroked. Cut the Base and a pair of Heads from the short pile fur. Cut four Ears from felt.

To make the Hedgehog

Stitch the Side Body darts. With right sides together, pin a matching Head piece to a Side Body as shown in Fig 2. Machine-stitch, easing the seam as you work. Work the other Head piece and Side Body in the same way.

Stitch the back seam A–B. Complete the body by sewing under the snout seam C–D, leaving A–C open for inserting the nose. Insert the base, leaving a gap for stuffing E–B–E. Turn the skin right side out, insert the eyes (see Fig 1, page 12), stuff and close the open seam.

Ears Topstitch two Ear pieces together on all three sides 3mm (⅛in) from the edge. Lay the Ear flat on the prickly fur with the tip facing towards the snout and just touching the Head/Side Body seam. Sew securely in place by oversewing between the fur and the base of the Ear, then Ladder-stitch between the Body and the back layer of Ear. This will pull the ear up. Make and attach a second Ear in the same way.

Finish the Hedgehog by making and attaching a black ball nose.

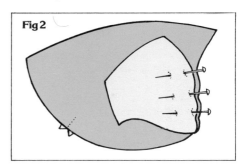

Fig 2 *Pin the Hedgehog's Head piece to the Side Body. Start pinning in the middle of the seam, then place pins vertically at each side*

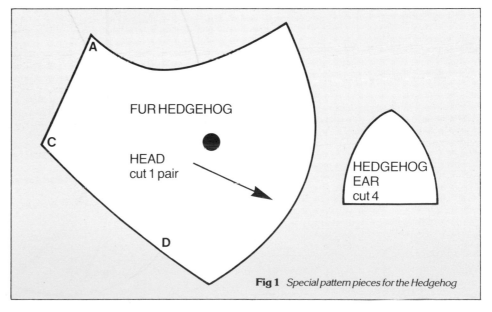

Fig 1 *Special pattern pieces for the Hedgehog*

FUR HEDGEHOG

HEAD
cut 1 pair

HEDGEHOG
EAR
cut 4

Ladybird

The Ladybird is an example of the versatility of simple patterns. More ideas for adaptations to the pattern are suggested on page 45.

Materials required
Finished size 18cm (7¼in) long
23cm (9in)-square of black short pile fur
23cm (9in)-square of red short pile fur
15cm *(6in)* square of black felt
12.5cm *(5in)* length of black bias binding
Pair of small black domed buttons
Small piece of white felt
50g *(2oz)* of stuffing

Making the pattern
From the trace-off pattern Fig 1 on page 17, trace the Side Body, taking note of the special cutting line at the 'neck'. From the trace-off pattern Fig 1 this page, trace the Head, Ladybird Base and the Spot. Make a set of card patterns. Transfer all relevant markings. A 6mm (¼in) seam allowance is included on all pattern pieces.

Cutting out
Cut a pair of Side Bodies from red fur. Cut the Head and Base from black fur as directed. Cut seven black felt spots.

Making the Ladybird
Stitch the Side Body darts. Stitch the Ladybird Head pieces to the body, as directed for working the Fur Hedgehog (Fig 2, page 21). Machine-stitch the centre back seam A–B.

Run a double gathering thread round the Head, I–G–F. Pull up the thread until the Head fits the end of the Base shape, F–G–F. Stitch the Head to the Base, evenly spreading the fullness and matching F–F, G–G, F–F.

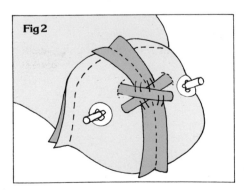

Fig 2 *Ladybird from the wrong side of the head showing the bias binding antennae crossed over the seam and stitched*

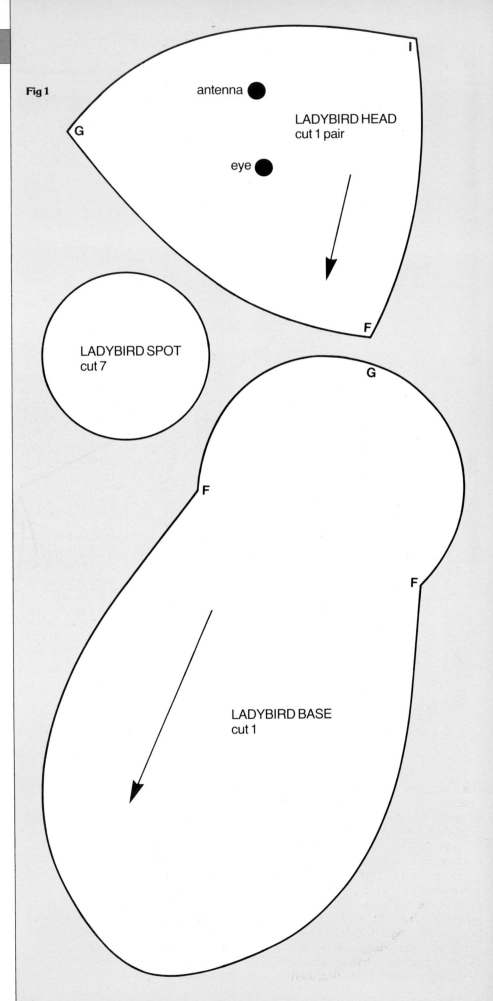

Fig 1

antenna

LADYBIRD HEAD
cut 1 pair

eye

G

F

LADYBIRD SPOT
cut 7

G

F

F

LADYBIRD BASE
cut 1

I

Working the Head

Fold the piece of bias binding along its length and machine-stitch to make a thin cord. Tie a knot at each end of the cord and trim the raw edges close. Cut the cord in half, making two antennae.

Pierce holes in Head for the antennae with a sharp pointed tool or scissors point, at the points marked on the Head pattern. Push an antenna through each hole from the right side, leaving about 2cm (¾in) protruding. Sew in place on the wrong side by catching the base of the antennae to the seam first, then securely to head where they pass through the hole (Fig 2).

Cut two circles of white felt, each slightly larger than the diameter of the eye button. Make a slit in the felt for the shank of the button to go through then stick the felt to the buttons by spreading a little clear adhesive on the back. When the adhesive has set, trim the felt, leaving a narrow edge surrounding the button. Secure the eyes to the Head by sewing them in place on the right side, approximately 12mm (½in) in front of the antennae.

Finishing

Make the Ladybird's spots by running a gathering thread around each black felt circle. Pull the gathering threads up tightly and fasten off the thread ends. Press the spots between the fingers, to flatten them and to spread the gathers. Hem the spots in place on the Ladybird's 'wings' (see picture).

Complete the Ladybird by stitching the Body to the Base leaving an opening E–E for stuffing. Turn the skin right side out, stuff and close the opening with Ladder stitch (Fig 1, page 10).

Whale

This charming soft toy has several new pattern pieces but uses the Base from the basic pattern on page 17.

Materials required

Finished size 23cm (9in) long
30cm (12in) of 46cm (18in)-wide
    polished short pile blue fur
23cm (9in) square of polished short pile
    grey fur
1 pair of 15mm (⅝in) blue safety eyes
75g (3oz) of stuffing

Making the pattern

From the trace-off pattern Fig 1 trace the Side Body, Upper Tail Fluke and Flipper. From the trace-off pattern Fig 1 page 17, trace the Base. Make a set of card patterns, cutting a Side Body, Flipper, Upper Tail Fluke and Base. Transfer all markings. A seam allowance of 6mm (¼in) is included on all pattern pieces.

Cutting out

Cut a pair of Side Bodies, one Tail Fluke and a pair of Flippers from the blue fur. Cut the Base and a pair of Flippers from the grey fur.

To make the Whale

Stitch a grey and blue Flipper together, right sides facing, leaving the straight edge open. Turn right side out, clean the seam (refer to page 9), then baste where indicated to the right side of the Side Body, with blue sides of fur together and raw edges level. (Flippers point backwards.) Sew in place. Make the second Flipper in same way and attach it to the other Side Body.

Stitch the Body darts, then with right sides together, stitch the centre top seam B–H. Insert the safety eyes (refer to Fig 1 page 12). Stitch the Base in place, checking that the Flippers are caught securely in the seams.

Spread the lower tail fluke apart (see pattern of Side Body) and lay the Upper Fluke on top right sides facing. Machine-stitch, breaking stitching at H and J so that the Body is not trapped in the seams. Turn the Body and Flukes right side out and stuff the main bulk of Body through opening J–D.

Finishing

Close the opening with Ladder stitch, starting at D and working towards the Flukes. Insert more stuffing as necessary. The Tail Flukes are not stuffed. Work some topstitches between the flukes to keep the stuffing out and also to keep them flat.

Work a row of Running stitches from J to H and pull them towards the body, to raise the Flukes and give more shape to the whale (see picture).

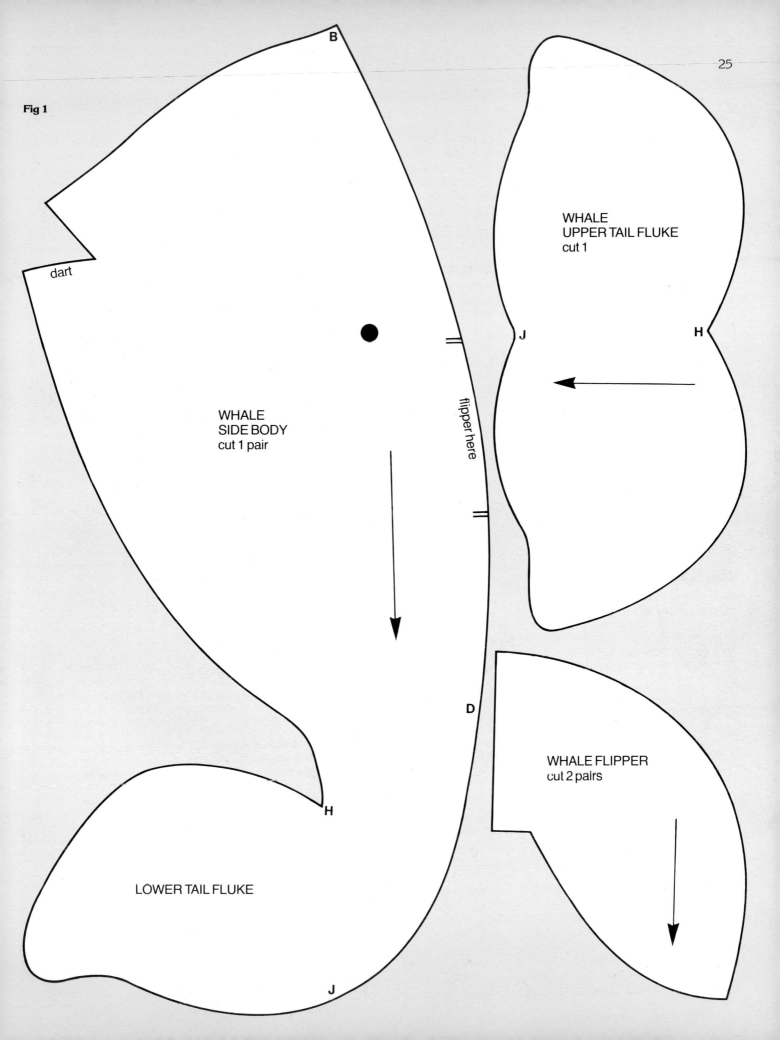

Fig 1

25

B

dart

WHALE
SIDE BODY
cut 1 pair

flipper here

WHALE
UPPER TAIL FLUKE
cut 1

J   H

D

WHALE FLIPPER
cut 2 pairs

H

LOWER TAIL FLUKE

B

J

Cuddly Animals

Three bears, a panda, a fox and a rabbit make up this collection of cuddly animals.
Teddy is especially cuddly, with his swing-hinged arms and legs, and so is panda who is
a colour variation of the teddy. The bear cub and fox introduce further pattern styles,
each one more demanding than the one before, while the challenging part of the rabbit
is to stuff him correctly so that he stands steady on his feet.

Teddy

Materials required
Finished size 35cm (14in) tall
60cm (24in) square of short pile fur
Small piece of contrasting fabric for sole
   and ear linings
200g (8oz) of stuffing
1 pair of 15mm (⅝in) amber safety eyes
1 skein of stranded embroidery cotton,
   Brown

Making the pattern
Make a set of card patterns from the
trace-off patterns on pages 28–29, 30–
31, transferring all details. Only half of
the Teddy Body is given. Make a full size
card pattern by tracing the shape onto
folded tracing paper, matching the fold
with the broken line on the pattern
marked 'place to fold'. Re-trace the
outline to obtain the whole pattern. Trace
the Teddy Body, Sole, Ear, Side Head,
Head Gusset, Arm and Leg. A seam
allowance of 6mm (¼in) is included on
all pieces.

Cutting out
Place the card patterns on the wrong
side of the fur and draw round using
chalk pencil, taking note of the pile
direction arrows. Cut out all pieces as
directed on the pattern. Cut the Sole and
Ear linings from contrasting fabric.

To make the Teddy
Make the Arms first. Place the Arm
pieces together in pairs and oversew the
edges before seaming. Leave the top
edges open. Turn the Arms right side out
and stuff them firmly to within 3cm
(1¼in) of the top. Use a pin to hold the
stuffing in place and to keep it away from
the opening (Fig 1). Make small pleats
on each side of the opening to reduce
the width of the arms, then oversew the
raw edges together in turn (Fig 1).

Inserting the Arms
On the Body piece, stitch the shoulder
dart A–B. Insert the Arm in the slot with
the paw facing forwards. Be prepared to
lengthen the arm slot to fit the Arm if
necessary. Open out the dart seam, fold
the shoulder down. Sew the Arm in place
(Fig 2). Leave a good portion of the arm
inside the Body, as this will ensure that it
is well secured. Insert the second Arm in
the same way.
 Turn the Body to the right side and
check that Arms are correctly positioned.
Remove the pin.

Making the Legs
Fold the Legs in half C–C and D–D and
seam each from C–D. Position the Sole
and baste in place. Hand-sew in place.
Turn the Leg right side out and stuff it
nearly to the top and fasten with a pin as
for the Arms. Press the top of the Leg flat,
with the seam centred and oversew the
raw edges together. Finish the second
Leg in the same way and check that a
pair has been made.

Inserting the Legs
Machine-stitch the stomach dart E–F
then position the Legs on either side of
the dart and with raw edges level. Baste.
The toes should point forward when the

Legs swing down. Close the lower part of
the centre back seam G–H. Press the
lower front and back edges together and
sew across the gap through all four
thicknesses of fur.
 If four thicknesses prove too bulky for
machine-stitching, sew the Legs to the
front only, then turn the skin right side
out and Ladder-stitch the back of the
Body to the back of the Legs.
 With the skin right side out, stuff the
lower part of the Body. Close the
remainder of the centre back seam with
Ladder stitch. Run a gathering thread
around the neck and pull it up sufficiently
to draw in the raw edges.

Making the Head
Place the two fur Ear pieces with right
sides together, baste then machine-stitch
all round the curved edge I–K. Cut into
the Ear at J, turn in and stitch the seam
allowance J–K.
 Close the Ear with Ladder stitch,
leaving the raw edges I–J open. Position
the Ear in the slot on the Head (see
pattern page 29), matching I–I and J–J,
and baste in place. Fold the side of the
Head over to bring the raw edges of the
slot together, then machine-stitch. Be
careful not to catch the free end of the
Ear at K in the seam.

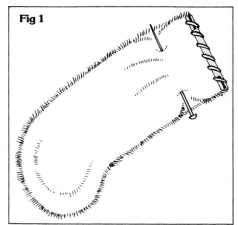

Fig 1

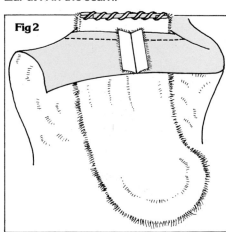

Fig 2

Machine-stitch the dart on the neck edge of the Head and complete the other side of the Head in the same way.

Place the Side Heads right sides together and stitch L–M. Insert the Head Gusset, matching L–L. Carefully baste one Side as far as N, then baste the other side. Turn the Head right side out and check its appearance before stitching in place. There should be no twisting.

Insert the safety eyes (refer to Fig 1, page 12). Stuff the Head firmly, rounding out the cheeks. Run a gathering thread around the neck and pull it up to draw the raw edges inwards. Ladder-stitch the Head to the Body.

The inside top edge of each Ear can be Ladder-stitched in place. Ears can either be pulled in to the top of the Head over the Gusset or turned forward along the Gusset seam.

Finishing

Embroider the nose with a block of Satin stitches, in brown embroidery cotton making the nose approximately 2cm (¾in) wide by 12mm (½in) deep. (Fig 3). Follow the instructions given for Fig 2b on page 13.

(When making Teddy Bears, dark fur toys can take a larger nose and light fur toys a smaller nose.)

Fig 1 *Insert a pin through the stuffed arm to keep the stuffing in place. Pleat in the sides to reduce the width. Oversew the top edges together*

Fig 2 *Fit the Arm to the shoulder through the slot. The paw should face forwards*

Fig 3 *Outline the Nose with Straight stitches, then fill in the shape with Satin stitches. Work the mouth with a long Straight stitch 1–2, then bring the needle out at 3 to catch down the long stitch. Insert the needle at 4, make 2 Straight sloping stitches at the mouth corners*

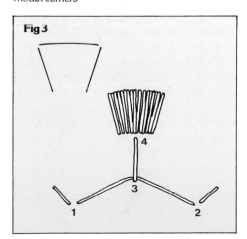

Fig 3

Cuddly Animals

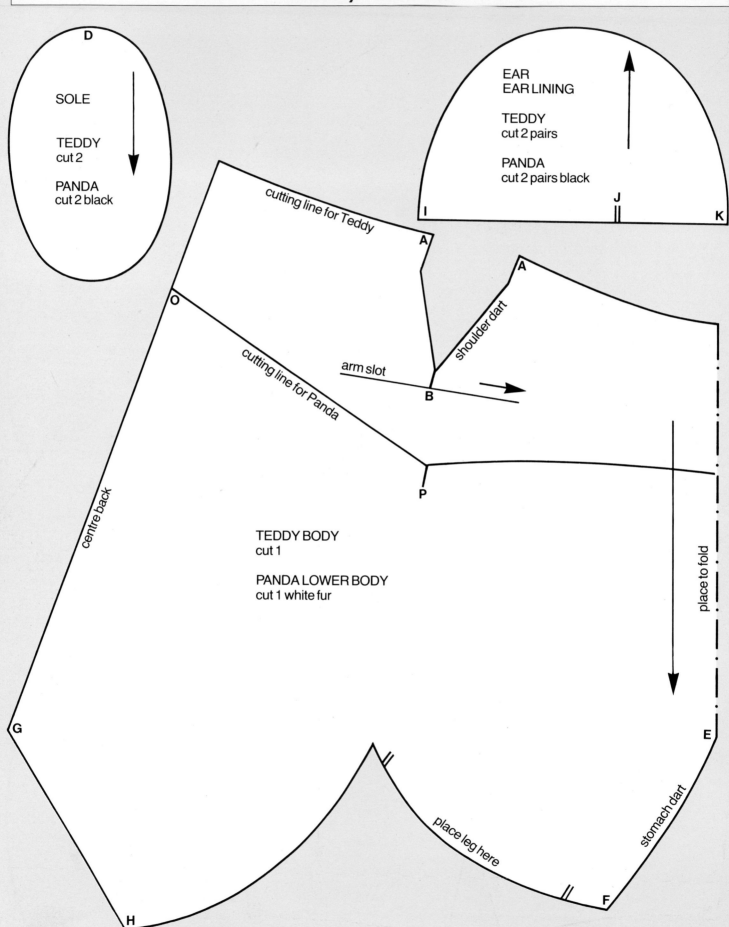

D

SOLE

TEDDY
cut 2

PANDA
cut 2 black

EAR
EAR LINING

TEDDY
cut 2 pairs

PANDA
cut 2 pairs black

I

J

K

cutting line for Teddy

A

A

shoulder dart

arm slot

B

O

cutting line for Panda

P

centre back

TEDDY BODY
cut 1

PANDA LOWER BODY
cut 1 white fur

place to fold

G

E

H

place leg here

stomach dart

F

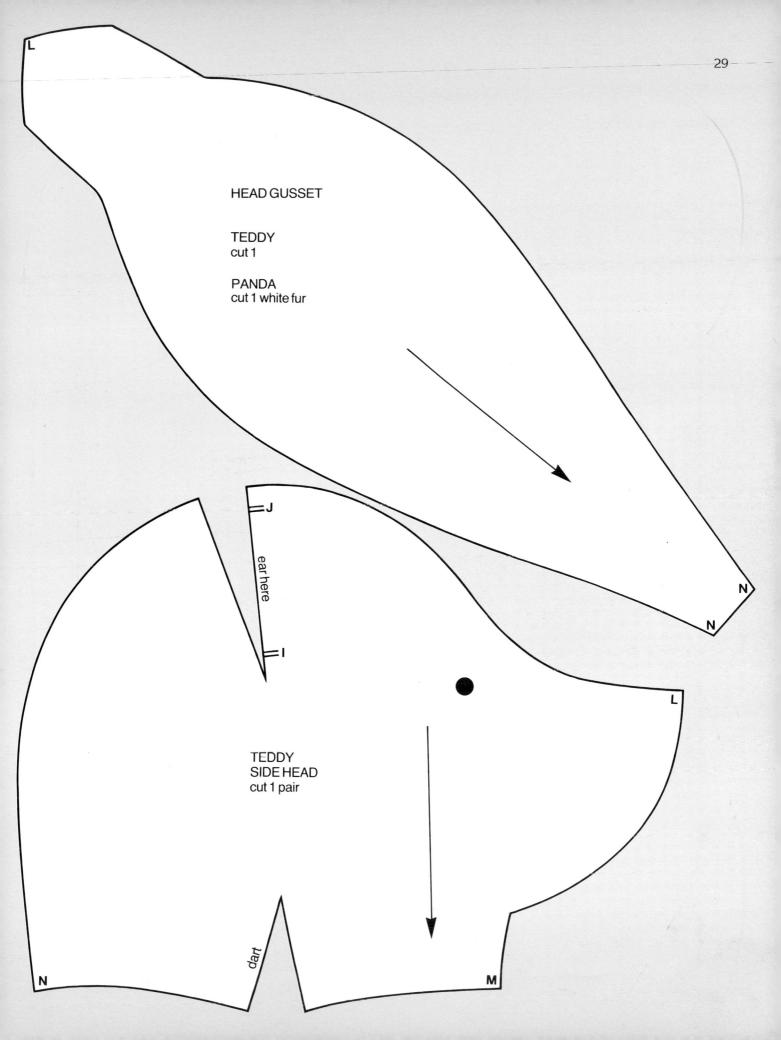

HEAD GUSSET

TEDDY
cut 1

PANDA
cut 1 white fur

L

J

ear here

I

N

N

L

TEDDY
SIDE HEAD
cut 1 pair

dart

N

M

Panda

The trace-off patterns for making the Panda are on pages 28–29 and 30–31.

Materials required

Finished size 35cm (14in) tall
46cm *(18in)* square of unpolished, short pile black fur
38cm *(15in)* × 46cm *(18in)* piece of unpolished, short pile white fur
Small piece of contrasting fabric, for soles
Stuffing and eyes as for Teddy
1 skein of stranded embroidery cotton, Black

Making the pattern

Make a set of card patterns from the trace-off patterns on pages 28–29, 30–31 transferring all relevant details. Note that the Panda Lower Body has a special cutting line. Only half of the Lower Body and Panda Chest patterns are given. To obtain a full size card pattern trace the shape on folded tracing paper, aligning the fold with the pattern edge marked 'place to fold'. Re-trace the outline to obtain the whole pattern. Trace the Panda Lower Body, Sole, Ears, Head Gusset, Arm, Leg, Chest, Head and Eye Patch. A seam allowance of 6mm *(¼in)* is included on all pieces.

Cutting out

Place the card patterns on the wrong side of the fur fabric, taking note of the pile direction arrows, and draw round the patterns with chalk pencil. Cut the Side Head, Head Gusset and Lower Body from white fur. Cut the Ears, Eye Patches, Arms, Legs and Chest from black fur. Cut the Soles from fabric.

To make the Panda

On the Lower Body piece, cut 5mm *(³⁄₁₆in)* into the seam allowance at P. Stitch the Chest to the Lower Body from O–P, P–P, P–O. Assemble the Panda following the instructions given for the Teddy on pages 26–27.

The Eye Patches require careful fitting as they must match on the head. Snip into the curved seam allowance T–S–R on the Panda Side Head pieces. With right sides together pin the Eye Patch, matching S–S. Pull gently and continue pinning matching raw edges and T–T and R–R, easing the seam. Baste and then Backstitch the Patch in position. Insert both Patches in the same way.

Continue making the Head by following the instructions for Teddy but give the Panda a black embroidered nose and mouth.

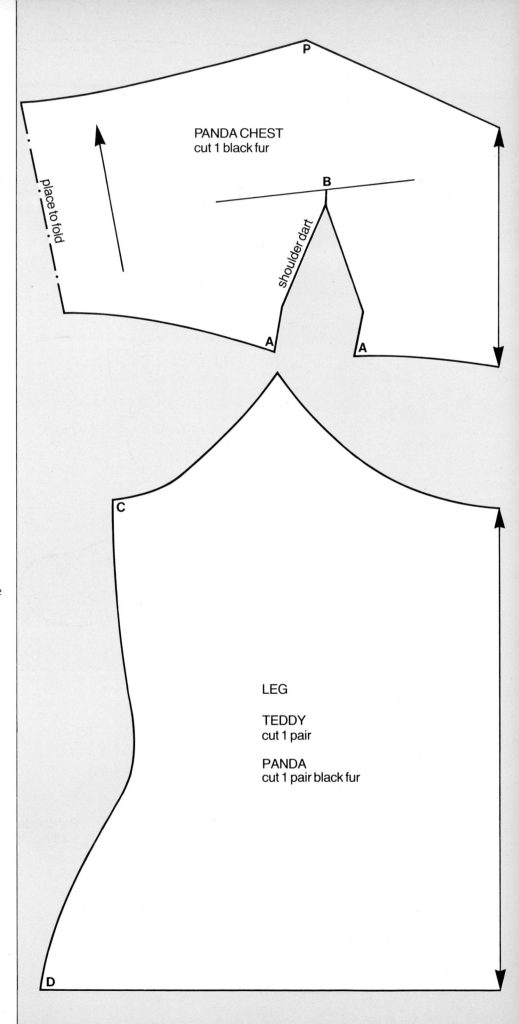

place to fold

P

PANDA CHEST
cut 1 black fur

B

shoulder dart

A   A

C

LEG

TEDDY
cut 1 pair

PANDA
cut 1 pair black fur

D

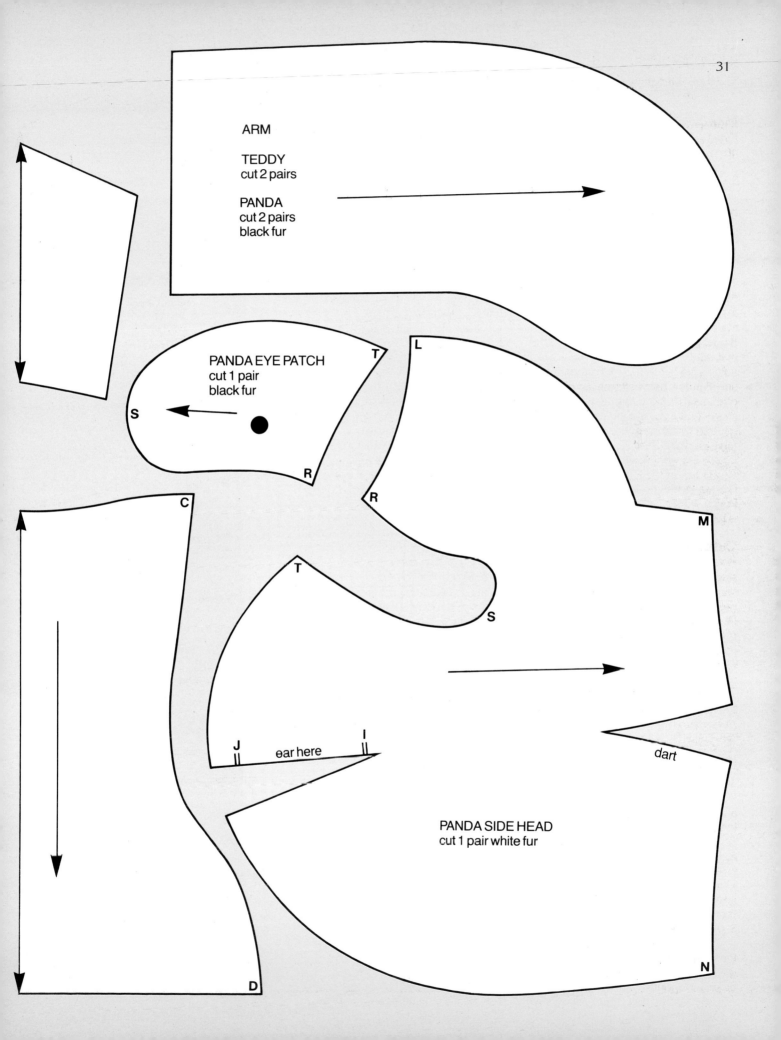

ARM

TEDDY
cut 2 pairs

PANDA
cut 2 pairs
black fur

PANDA EYE PATCH
cut 1 pair
black fur

T

L

S

R

R

C

T

S

M

J ear here I

dart

PANDA SIDE HEAD
cut 1 pair white fur

D

N

31

Bear Cub

In this pattern, the body has an inset piece for the front enabling the toy to sit firmly. The trace-off patterns are on pages 34–35.

Materials required

Finished size 18cm (7in) tall
46cm *(18in)* square of short pile fur
15cm *(6in)* square of fleece for sole and
  ear linings
1 pair of 15mm *(⅝in)* amber safety eyes
50g *(2oz)* of stuffing
Stranded embroidery cotton

Making the pattern

From the trace-off patterns on pages 34–35 trace all the shapes and make a set of card patterns. Transfer all markings. A seam allowance of 6mm *(¼in)* is included on all pieces.

Cutting out

Place the card patterns on the wrong side of the fur fabric, taking note of the pile direction arrows. Note that the Front Head can be cut either with the pile stroking back from the Snout or down from the Ears. Decide which you prefer, then cut a pair as instructed. Cut a pair of Front Heads, a pair of Back Heads, a pair of Front Bodies, a pair of Side Bodies, four Ears, one Base and one Snout. Cut two Soles from fleece.

To make the Bear Cub

On the Front Body pieces, fold the Arms and Legs to the right side and stitch the contour darts on the dotted line (see pattern). These bring the limbs forward and help the Cub to sit properly. Trim the fabric away close to the seam to release

tension in the darts.
   Stitch the Front Bodies together down the centre front A–B.
   Stitch the Side Bodies together from C–D, then position the Base and stitch in place D–E on each side.
   Match the completed Front Body to the Side Bodies. Baste the Arms together, making sure that the pile is tucked in away from the seam. Stitch the Front and Side Bodies together from the neck, around the arms and to the foot at F. Stitch from the bottom of the foot to E on each side. Leave the seam between E–E open.
   Clip the corners at the top of the Arms and between the Arms and Legs.
   Match the Sole to the foot at F and baste in place before sewing by hand.
   Turn the completed Body right side out. Check that the legs sit forward and if necessary resew deeper contour darts to achieve the correct position. Turn wrong side out and close the seam E–E. Turn the skin right side out again and stuff the body firmly, making sure that the Cub sits comfortably and has a rounded stomach. Close the back opening with Ladder stitch. Run a gathering thread around the neck and draw it up to roll the raw edges inwards.

Making the Head

Stitch the Front Heads together G–H. Open out to position the Snout. Stitch the Snout in place from the centre at H to J on each side in turn, easing the seam. Take care because the snout can easily twist to one side in working.
   Fold the Head in half down the centre front matching K–K, J–J and L–L. Stitch from the tip of the nose K down to neck edge L (Fig 1). To close the opening at

the tip of the nose, open the seam at K and press the raw edges together so that K and M come together. Stitch across the opening as shown (Fig 2).
   Stitch the Back Heads together down the centre back. Baste the Ears together

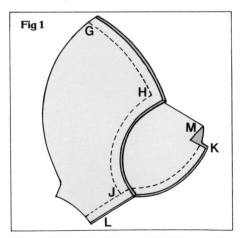

Fig 1 *Fold the Head in half and finish the seam K-J-L. Stitch from the nose to the neck*

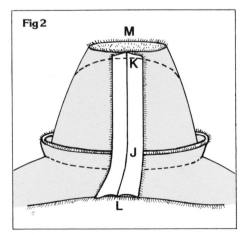

Fig 2 *Close the opening at the nose by pressing K and M together and stitching*

in pairs then machine-stitch. Turn right side out, clean the seams then baste in position on the Head as shown on the pattern. Stitch the Front and Back Heads together. Turn the completed Head right side out and check the position of the eyes before inserting them (refer to Fig 1, page 12 for the techniques).

Stuff the Snout firmly first and hold the stuffing in place by working a criss-cross web of stitches between the seam formed by stitching J—H—J. Continue stuffing the Head. Ladder-stitch the Head to the Body. Embroider a nose and mouth similar in shape to that of the Teddy (Fig 3, page 27) but smaller.

Instructions for making the Fox are on pages 36-37

Cuddly Animals

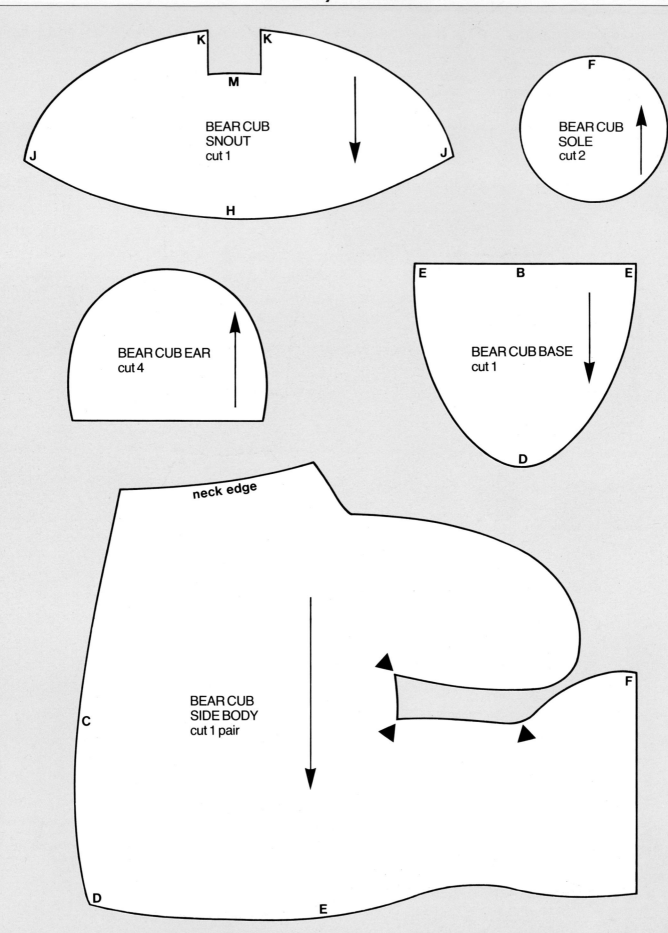

BEAR CUB
SNOUT
cut 1

K   K

M

J   J

H

F

BEAR CUB
SOLE
cut 2

BEAR CUB EAR
cut 4

E   B   E

BEAR CUB BASE
cut 1

D

neck edge

BEAR CUB
SIDE BODY
cut 1 pair

C

F

D   E

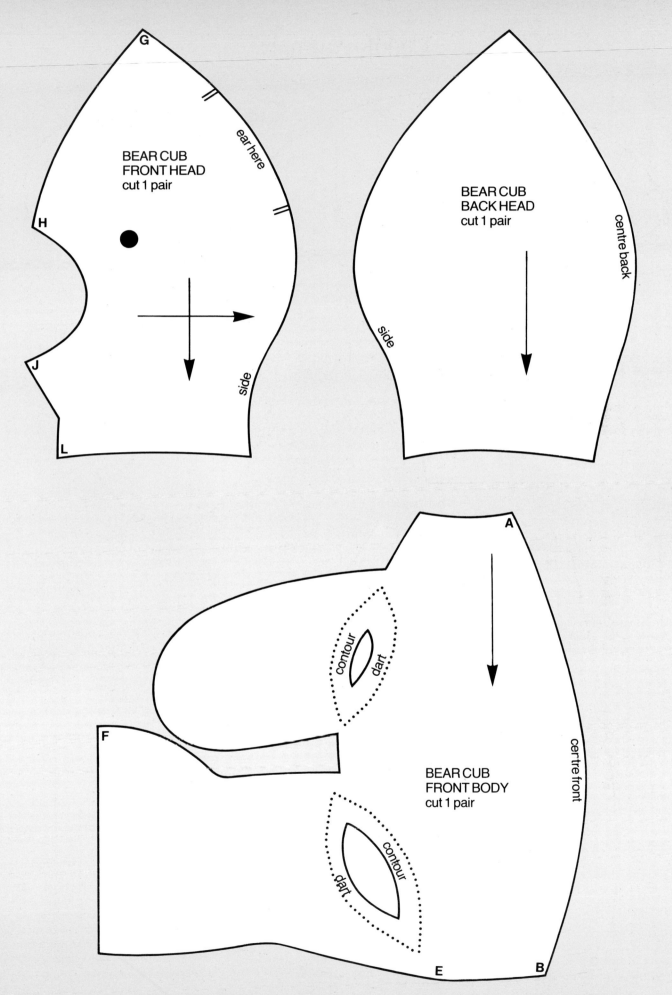

G

BEAR CUB
FRONT HEAD
cut 1 pair

ear here

H

side

J

L

BEAR CUB
BACK HEAD
cut 1 pair

centre back

side

A

contour

dart

BEAR CUB
FRONT BODY
cut 1 pair

centre front

F

contour

dart

E

B

Fox

The Fox is pictured with the Bear Cub on page 33. The trace-off patterns for the Fox toy continue from page 37 to pages 38–39.

Materials required

Finished size 28cm (11in) high and 40cm (16in) long
46cm *(18in)* × 68cm *(27in)* piece of short pile rust fur
30cm *(12in)* square of short pile white fur
15cm *(6in)* square of black fur
15cm (6in) square of contrasting fabric for soles
150g *(6oz)* of stuffing
1 pair of 15mm *(⅝in)* amber safety eyes
18mm *(¾in)* animal safety nose
Scrap of brown felt, for eye backing
Stranded embroidery cotton, Black

Making the pattern

Make a set of card patterns from the trace-off patterns on pages 37, 38 and 39 transferring all details. A seam allowance of 6mm *(¼in)* is included on all pieces.

Cutting out

Four different fabrics are used to make the Fox, so take care when laying out the pattern pieces.

Cut a pair of Ears from black fur and Front and Back Soles from the contrasting fabric. The Cheeks, Chin, Front Ears and Tail Tip are cut from white fur. All the other pieces are cut from rust fur. Cut two Eye Backings from brown felt.

To make the Fox

Stitch the Inside Back Legs together M–N, then stitch them to each Side Body in turn O–P, Q–N leaving P–Q open for the Back Soles.

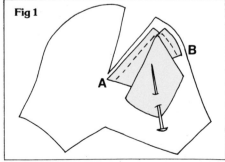

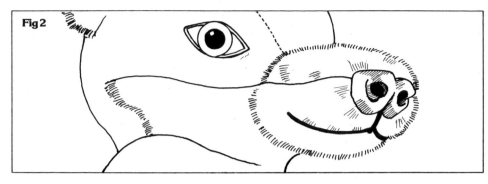

Fig 2 *Embroider a mouth on the Fox, following the lines shown here*

Stitch Inside Front Legs together R–M, then stitch them to each Side Body in turn S–T and U–O leaving T–U open for the Front Soles. Stitch the Inside Front Legs to the Inside Back Legs O–M–O.

Insert the Soles basting then machine-stitching, and breaking the stitching at T–U–P–Q so that the seams are not trapped. Turn the skin right side out and check the appearance for roundness and realism before turning to the wrong side and stitching the centre back seam down the body and across the base to N.

Clip the corners and turn the completed skin right side out for stuffing.

Stuffing the Fox

Begin by stuffing each Front Leg first as a pair so that they match, then the Back Legs, working up towards the Chest. Keep turning the body as you stuff and check from time to time that the animal sits firmly. Remember that the Front Legs sit between the Back Legs. Try not to over-stuff the Chest as this may push the Legs forward and upset the balance.

When you are satisfied with the shape of the body, run a gathering thread around the neck and pull it up slightly, drawing the raw edges together.

Clip into the seam allowance of the Tail Tip piece as shown on the pattern. Baste and then machine-stitch the Tail Tip to the Tail, wrong sides and matching V–V, W–W. When both sides of the Tail are completed, stitch them together leaving the straight edge open. Turn the Tail right side out and stuff it lightly. Clean all the seams, turn in the raw edges and Ladder-stitch the Tail in place at the lower back of the Body.

Making the Head

Place a black and white Ear piece together with right sides facing and sew round the curved edge, leaving the bottom edge open A–B. Turn the Ear right side out and clean the seams. Oversew the bottom edges together.

Then pin along the front edge of the slit on the Head with right sides together, matching A–A. Baste. The black back of the Ear should be uppermost. Turn the Ear forward to lie along the Gusset side of the Head, matching B–B. Clip into the seam allowance so that the Ear turns forward. Pin the tip of the Ear down so that it does not become trapped in the seam (Fig 1).

Bring the edges of the slit together right sides facing and stitch from A to the edge. Work the second Ear in the same way.

Stitch the Head Gusset to the Head matching C–C along one side first and stitching to D. Repeat on other side. Now position the Upper Snout and stitch E–C–C–E.

Sew the cheeks together F–G. On the Chin piece, pin and baste the edges H–H–h–H together, right sides facing. Machine-stitch. Stitch the Chin to Cheeks matching E–E on each side and H–F in the centre.

Pin the completed Lower Head to the Head, matching the tip of the Snout at J and working back through E–K on each side in turn. Baste in place and check that it is not twisted before stitching. Finish stitching the Head by bringing L to L and stitching to form a dart.

Turn the completed Head skin right side out. Thread felt Eye Backings onto the shanks of the eyes, then fix them in place, making sure that the felt pieces lie correctly before pushing the washer home. Fix the nose in place, again checking that it is fixed the right way up.

Stuff the Head carefully, shaping the Cheeks. Run a gathering thread around the neck edge of the cheeks from L–L. This will accentuate the Cheeks. Ladder-stitch the Head to the Body with the Fox looking over his shoulder (see picture). Embroider a mouth as in Fig 2.

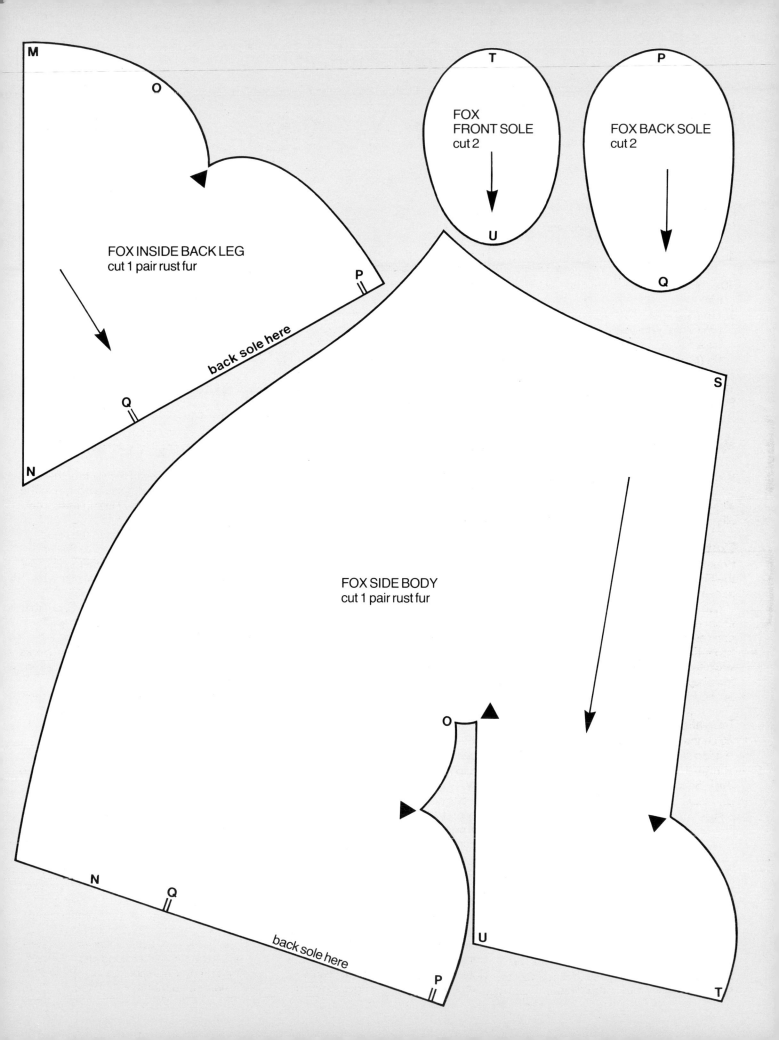

FOX INSIDE BACK LEG
cut 1 pair rust fur

back sole here

FOX SIDE BODY
cut 1 pair rust fur

back sole here

FOX
FRONT SOLE
cut 2

FOX BACK SOLE
cut 2

Cuddly Animals

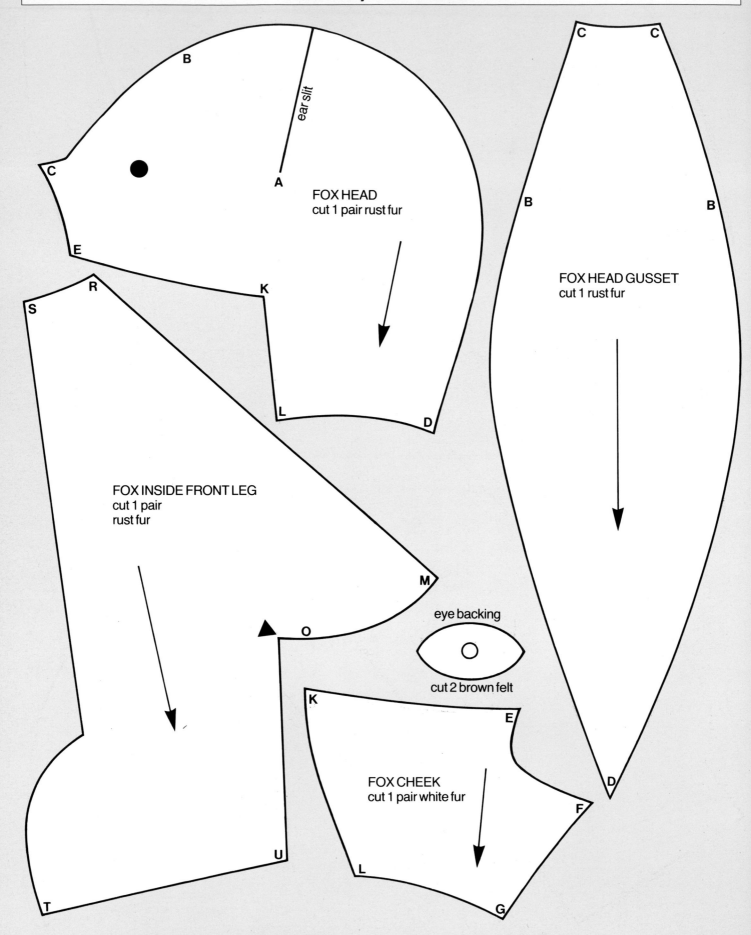

ear slit

B

C

E

A

FOX HEAD
cut 1 pair rust fur

K

L

D

C C

B B

FOX HEAD GUSSET
cut 1 rust fur

D

R

S

FOX INSIDE FRONT LEG
cut 1 pair
rust fur

M

O

eye backing

cut 2 brown felt

K

E

F

FOX CHEEK
cut 1 pair white fur

U

L

G

T

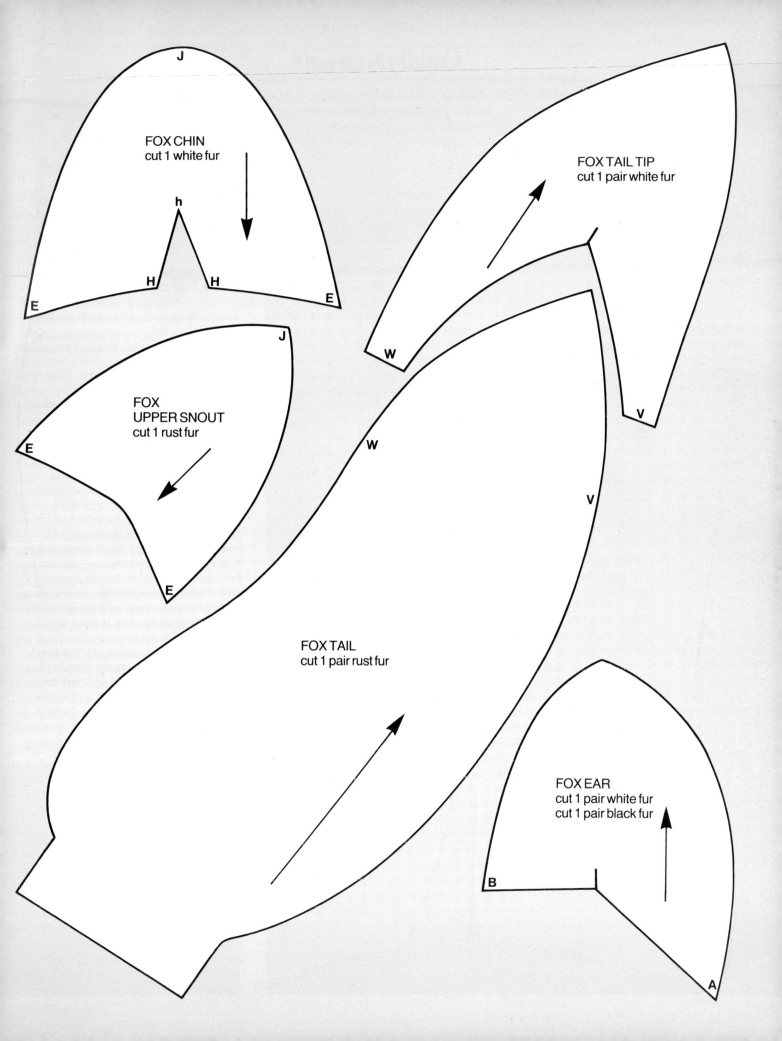

FOX CHIN
cut 1 white fur

J

h

H   H

E   E

FOX TAIL TIP
cut 1 pair white fur

W

V

FOX
UPPER SNOUT
cut 1 rust fur

J

E

W

V

E

FOX TAIL
cut 1 pair rust fur

FOX EAR
cut 1 pair white fur
cut 1 pair black fur

B

A

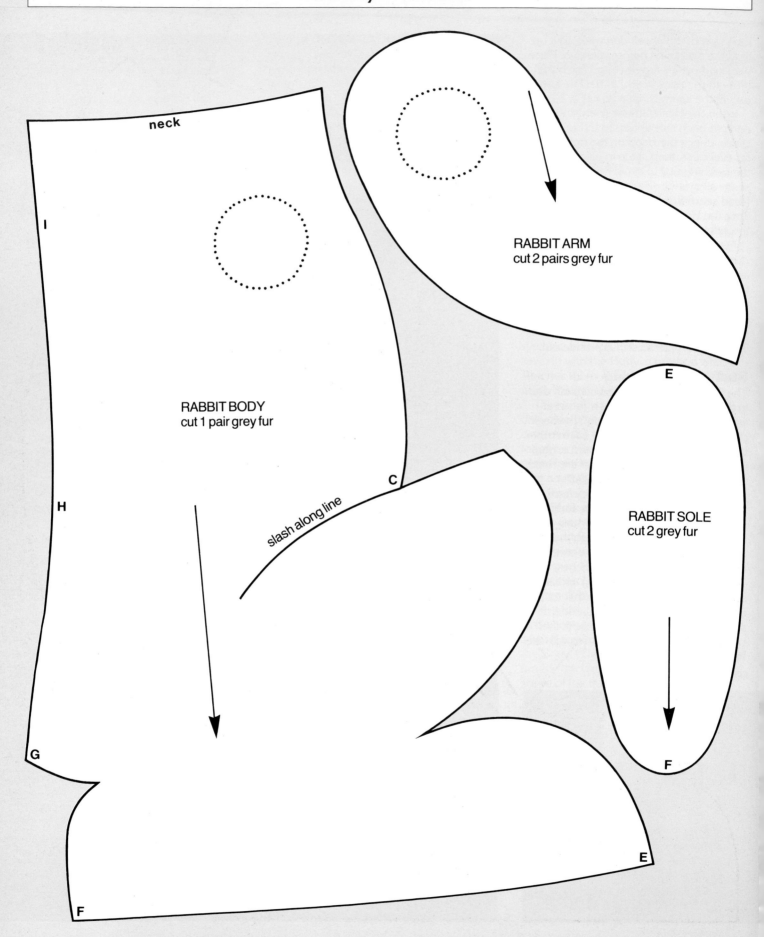

neck

RABBIT ARM
cut 2 pairs grey fur

I

RABBIT BODY
cut 1 pair grey fur

E

RABBIT SOLE
cut 2 grey fur

H

C

slash along line

G

F

E

F

F

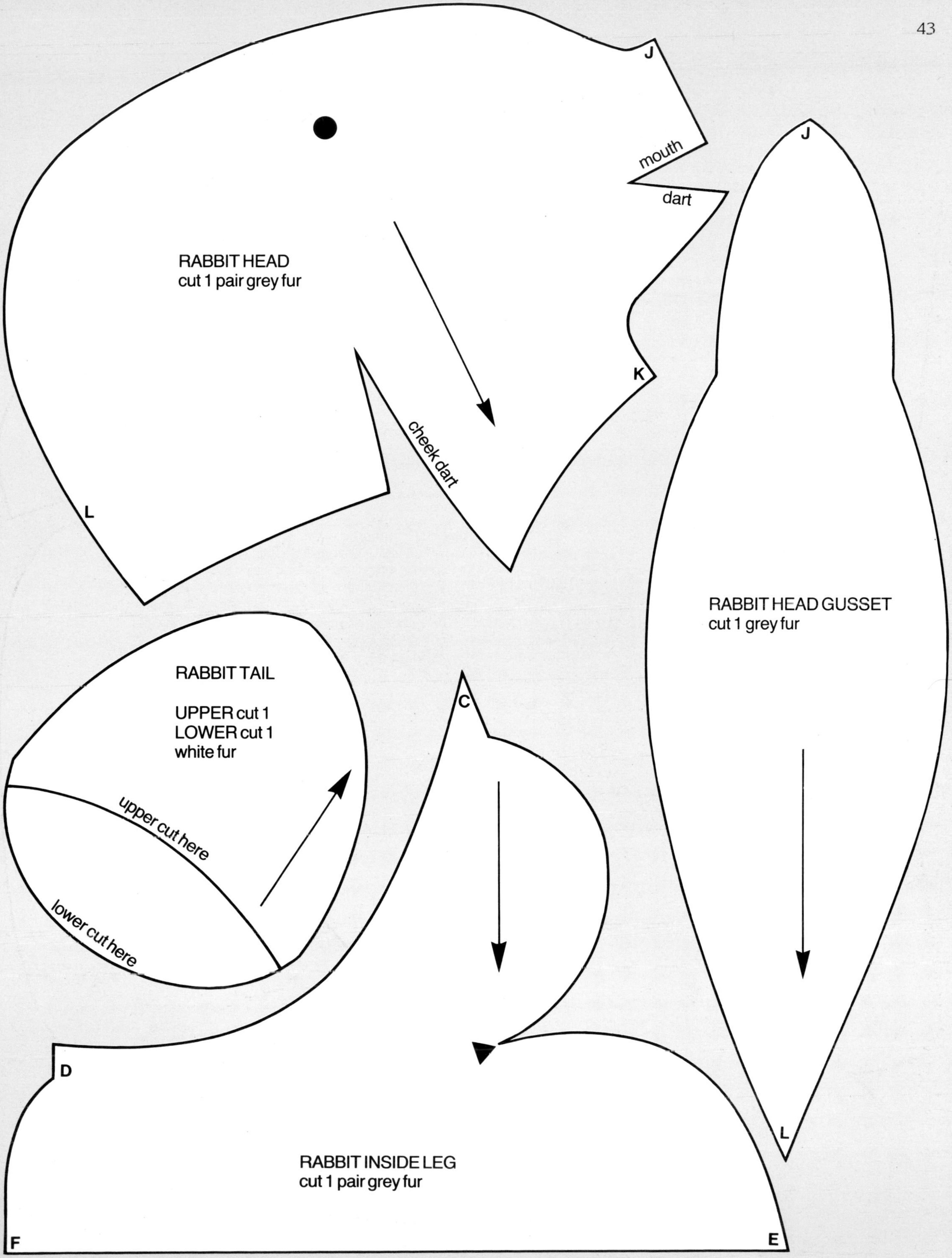

RABBIT HEAD
cut 1 pair grey fur

mouth

dart

cheek dart

J

K

L

RABBIT HEAD GUSSET
cut 1 grey fur

J

L

RABBIT TAIL

UPPER cut 1
LOWER cut 1
white fur

upper cut here

lower cut here

C

D

RABBIT INSIDE LEG
cut 1 pair grey fur

F

E

44

Stitch the Tail pieces together, leaving the bottom end open. Turn right side out, insert a little stuffing, then draw up the raw edges and Ladder-stitch the Tail in place at the lower edge of the back. The Upper Tail lies next to the Body.

Ears Place a pair of Ears together and stitch around the curved edges. Turn right side out and clean the seam. Turn in the raw edges at the base, then fold the Ear in half and oversew the edges together at the base. Make a second Ear in the same way but check that you fold to make a pair. Ladder-stitch the Ears to the Head in the desired position. Check that the folds of the Ears are placed towards the centre top of Head (Fig 4).

Embroider a nose following Fig 5, using six strands of embroidery thread. Finally, using a length of button thread in a long needle, take a stitch from under the chin through the inside of the head up to the corner of an eye and back again to the chin. Pull it up to recess the eye into a socket, fasten securely then sink the eye on the other side in the same way. Tie off the threads and Backstitch the ends into the neck seam.

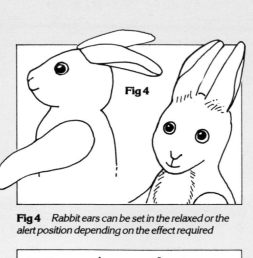

Fig 4 Rabbit ears can be set in the relaxed or the alert position depending on the effect required

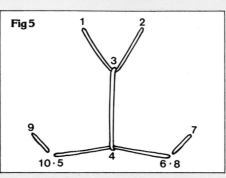

Fig 5 Working the nose and mouth: bring the needle out at 1 and insert it at 2. Bring it out at 3 and catch the loop of thread 1–2. Insert the needle at 4, bring the needle out at 5 and insert it at 6, taking the thread under the thread at 4. Working stitches 7–8 and 9–10 for a happy mouth

RABBIT FRONT BODY GUSSET
cut 1 pair white fur

centre front

RABBIT EAR
cut 1 pair grey fur
cut 1 pair white fur

fold on this line

Variations on the patterns

Many of the patterns in this book can be used as the basis for more toy ideas. An indication of this has already been shown by the variety of animals which can be made from adapting the basic patterns in Chapter two, making the Teddy in different colours to make a Panda and then by interchanging different parts of the dolls in Chapter 4. Think along these lines with every pattern you use and several more adaptations should spring to mind.

All animals are clearly recognisable by their individual features. Closely related animals have similar features and will only differ from one another in a few details. Always try to work out just those few necessary details which identify an animal and incorporate them in your new design. For instance, the Ladybird pattern when made in brown fur fabric, has the outline of a very simple rabbit, minus legs. It only needs a pair of long ears and a small bobble tail to confirm the identification. Having established ears and tail as the identifying details you can proceed further. Make the ears extra long, turn them down so that they lie against the side of the head and you have made a Lop-eared rabbit. Use a medium-length white fur for the body and you have an Angora. This breed of domestic rabbit can be more positively identified if you shave the lower ears and leave long tufts of fur on the tips. Or, make a Dutch rabbit, by using black and white fur.

The same Ladybird pattern can be developed in quite a different way. Pointed ears, eyes with slit pupils, a long tail and a set of whiskers will transform this animal into a cat. Simple fore limbs could be made and sewn in place on the outside of the body as for the Mole. Then imagine the same pattern made in dark brown fur with small rounded ears, black beady eyes and a velvet paddle for a tail and you have a beaver.

A colour change is an easier alteration to make. Look at the Bear Cubs and you will see that the blue bear has white sides, ear linings, snout and stomach. This colour change is achieved by cutting the inside legs and arms away from the front body pattern and redrawing these three pattern pieces with a new 6mm (¼in)

seam allowance on the cut edges. Cut the inside arms and legs in blue fur and sew them to a white fur stomach, then proceed as directed.

The body of the Fox has a typical pose that would suit other animals, such as dogs and cats. Similarly, the pattern for the Rabbit will produce a posture which would suit a squirrel, a woodchuck or a mouse. For these animals it is really a matter of adding different ears and tails and then redrawing the heads to make them slightly more pointed at the nose.

Adapting Doll patterns

The dolls can also be varied. Make a long-limbed Lara, using Ziggy's pattern. Shape her hands and give her fingers as described for the Topys-Turvy sisters, then sew across the elbows so that the arms bend. Give her a different hair style, dress her in a long dress without the bodice frill, add length to the pants and finish her off with a pinafore to make an old-fashioned girl.

An easy nightdress for her can be made using the clown costume. Place the inside leg seam on a fold and

continue the seam up to the neck edge without cutting any fabric to make the centre front of a nightdress. Do the same thing for the back. A slit opening down from the neck will enable you to fit the nightdress on the doll. Neaten the opening with a narrow hem or a strip of bias binding continued around the neck to make a front tie. By using patterns in this way you can start to build up a wardrobe for your doll.

Adapt the idea of the Topsy-Turvy doll and at one end make a grandmother wearing a nightie. A fox head on the other end can be the wolf. Dress Lara in a red cape and hood and you will have a storybook doll trio which will provide hours of fun.

The same upside down doll could be made with only one doll. Close the bottom of the dress to make a bag, make a new opening in the back of the skirt and you have a nightdress case.

And finally, glove puppets are among the easiest toys to use and have great play potential as knockabout characters. The heads of the Bears, Fox and Rabbit can all be used on a three-fingered glove.

Make a rabbit or a cat from the Ladybird pattern

A dog can be adapted from the Fox pattern

Rag Dolls

The rag dolls in this chapter are made in the time-honoured way, with stitched bodies, embroidered faces or felt features and yarn hair. Use your imagination to modify the basic doll, changing the clothing, altering the hair style or embroidering different expressions.
This will make your dolls quite special creations.

Lara

Lara sits up properly because she has a special seating dart worked into the back of the body. Both Lara and Ziggy the Clown are made from the same basic pattern.

Materials required for doll
Finished size 42cm (16½in) tall
46cm *(18in)* of 91cm *(36in)*-wide calico
170g *(6oz)* stuffing
25g *(1oz)* of cream knitting yarn
Stranded embroidery cottons Blue, White, Black, Brown, Pink
Red pencil
Strong, flexible wire, wire cutters

Materials required for clothes
50cm *(20in)* of 91cm *(36in)*-wide white cotton fabric
50cm *(20in)* of 91cm *(36in)*-wide cotton lawn fabric
152cm *(60in)* of trimming for dress
120cm *(48in)* of broderie anglaise
30cm *(12in)* square of felt for shoes
56cm *(22in)* of narrow elastic
5 press fasteners
2 small buttons for shoes
15cm *(6in)* of 6mm *(¼in)*-wide ribbon

Making the pattern
Trace the Doll Body patterns and the clothing patterns from the trace-off patterns on pages 49, 50, 52 and 53. Take note of the special cutting lines for Lara. The Body Front and Body Back are given in one outline on page 50. These should be traced off as separate patterns. Make card patterns.

   Card patterns can be made from the clothes tracings or the traced patterns can be cut out and pinned to fabric in the usual way.

   A 6mm *(¼in)* seam allowance is included on all pattern pieces.

   Make a separate tracing of the Doll's features (see pattern on page 49).

Cutting out the Doll
Draw round the Head card pattern on double calico fabric and cut out the Head pieces. Cut the Body Front and Body Back from single fabric. Draw round the Arm and Leg patterns twice each on double fabric but do not cut out at this stage.

Cutting out the Clothes
Dress Cut Lara's Dress Bodice from lawn fabric. Cut two Backs and cut one Front on the fold of fabric.

   Cut the Dress skirt piece from lawn 91 × 20cm *(36 × 8in)*. Cut two Bodice frills each 45 × 6cm *(18 × 2½in)*. Cut a bias strip for the Neck edge 19 × 2.5cm *(7½ × 1in)*. Cut two Sleeves placing the pattern to folded fabric.
Petticoat The Petticoat is cut from and lined with cotton fabric. Thus, cut out the Bodice pieces twice. Cut Four Backs and cut two Fronts placing the pattern to the fold of fabric. Cut the Petticoat Skirt 70 × 15cm *(28 × 6in)*.
Pants Cut the Pants from cotton fabric, placing the pattern to the fold of fabric as directed. The finished waist edge will slope from the Back to the Front.

   Cut two Sole Shoes and two Uppers from felt.

Making the Doll
Make the Arms first. Without cutting the fabric, stitch two Arms pieces together, right sides facing, stitching 6mm *(¼in)* inside the pencilled line. Leave the top straight edge open. Cut out the Arms on the pencilled line and clip between the thumbs and fingers. Turn right side out and stuff the Arms firmly up to the line marked on the pattern. Hold the stuffing in position by inserting a needle through the fabric. Use a fine needle so that the calico is not marked. Turn in the raw edges at the top of the arms by about 2.5cm *(1in)*. Make a small pleat on each side. Oversew the edges together.

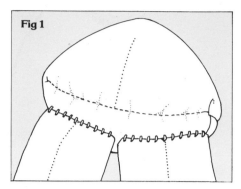

Fig 1 *Sew the Doll's legs to the Body Front with Ladder stitch*

Making the Legs

Pin and baste pairs of Legs pieces together. Stitch the Front and Back Leg seams stitching 6mm (¼in) inside the pencilled line leaving the leg open at the foot between A and B.

Cut out the legs on the pencil line. To shape the toes bring A and B together and oversew the seam, rounding off the toes. Turn the completed Legs right side out and stuff them up to the line marked on the pattern. Fasten to hold the stuffing in position (as for the Arms) then turn under the seam allowance on the top edge and oversew the edges together.

Stitch the seating dart on the lower edge of Body Back, then stitch front and Back Bodies together on the sides, across the shoulders and around the neck hump. Turn right side out and stuff very firmly, especially the neck. Close the opening at the bottom using Ladder stitch.

Position the tops of the Legs on the Body Front as indicated by a broken line on the pattern. Turn the Legs up so that the toes point towards the Head and sew the backs of the Legs securely to the Body with Ladder stitch (see Fig 1). For extra strength, Ladder-stitch across the front of the legs. The Doll Body should sit easily.

Making the Head

Stitch the two crown dartrs on both the Front and Back Head pieces. Stitch the neck darts. Sew the head pieces together right side facing, being careful to keep the cheek curves equal on both sides.

Leave the neck edge open and turn the Head right side out. Turn under the neck edge and baste the turning. Stuff the Head firmly. Work a thumb up through the Head stuffing to make a cavity large enough to fit the Body's neck hump. Carefully push the Head onto the

Body and Ladder-stitch in place, with the neck darts at the centre front, and back and side seams matching the shoulder seams. Remove the basting thread from the neck.

Arms

Position the Arms on the shoulders and sew them in place. The Arms should hang down from the shoulder, with the hands reaching the tops of the Legs. If the Arms will not hang properly or are too long, open up the tops and remove a little stuffing then adjust the fit.

Working the features

Position and pin the tracing of the features onto the front of the head with the pencilled side of the tracing against the calico. Gently draw over the outline to produce a thin pencil line on the fabric. Check frequently to ensure that the alignment is correct. A plastic eraser will remove unwanted marks.

All thread ends should start on the side of the Head, where they will be hidden by the hair. With 3 strands of embroidery cotton in the needle embroider the blue iris, using long and short Straight stitches radiating from the centre of the eye. Work black pupils on top of the blue in Satin stitch. Work the whites of the eyes with a few Straight stitches. Outline the top of the eyes in brown Stem stitch. Add a few Straight stitch eyelashes at each side. Use the same brown thread to work eyebrows in Stem stitch. Work the nostrils with two very small Straight stitches. Embroider the mouth in pink Stem stitch. Finish the face by colouring the cheeks with red pencil, the point held flat against the fabric and moved in a circular motion.

Making the hair

Bend the piece of wire as shown in Fig 2, so that the arms are about 5cm (2in) apart. Cut a piece of card as shown in Fig 2 to make a 'bridge' to hold the wire arms in position. Wind the cream-coloured yarn around the wire frame, working from the bridge down towards the bend in the wire. When sufficient yarn has been wound, work Backstitches through the middle of the wound yarn and then push the stitched yarn towards the cut ends of the frame, removing the 'bridge' when necessary. Continue winding and sewing through the yarn, making a long continuous strip of double curls. Use up all the yarn.

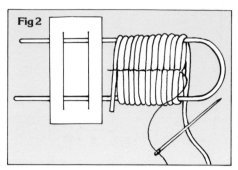

Fig 2 *The bent wire frame and the cardboard bridge. Wind yarn round the wire then secure the loops with Backstitches worked through the strands*

Fold the strip of curls in the middle and position this on the front of the Head at the spot marked X on the pattern. Backstitch half the curls in place on one side of the Head, following the placement line (the broken line on the pattern) and out to the side then around the back of the neck and up the back of the head to the crown. Make sure that no gaps are left. Backstitch the remaining half of the curls to the other side of the Head. Tie a small bow in the ribbon and sew the bow in place on the front hair line (see picture).

Making the Clothes
Pants

Turn up and press a narrow hem to the right side along the lower edge of both pieces of the Pants.

Fold under the raw edge of the broderie anglaise and press. Cut a length of broderie anglaise to fit each leg of the Pants, then machine-stitch it in place over the raw edge of the folded hem. Using machine zigzag stitch, stitch the elastic along the guide lines of each leg, stretching it as you stitch.

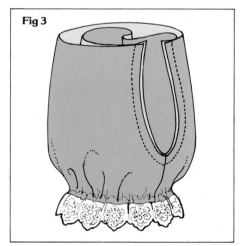

Fig 3 *First stage of the french seam joining the Pant's centre front and centre back seam*

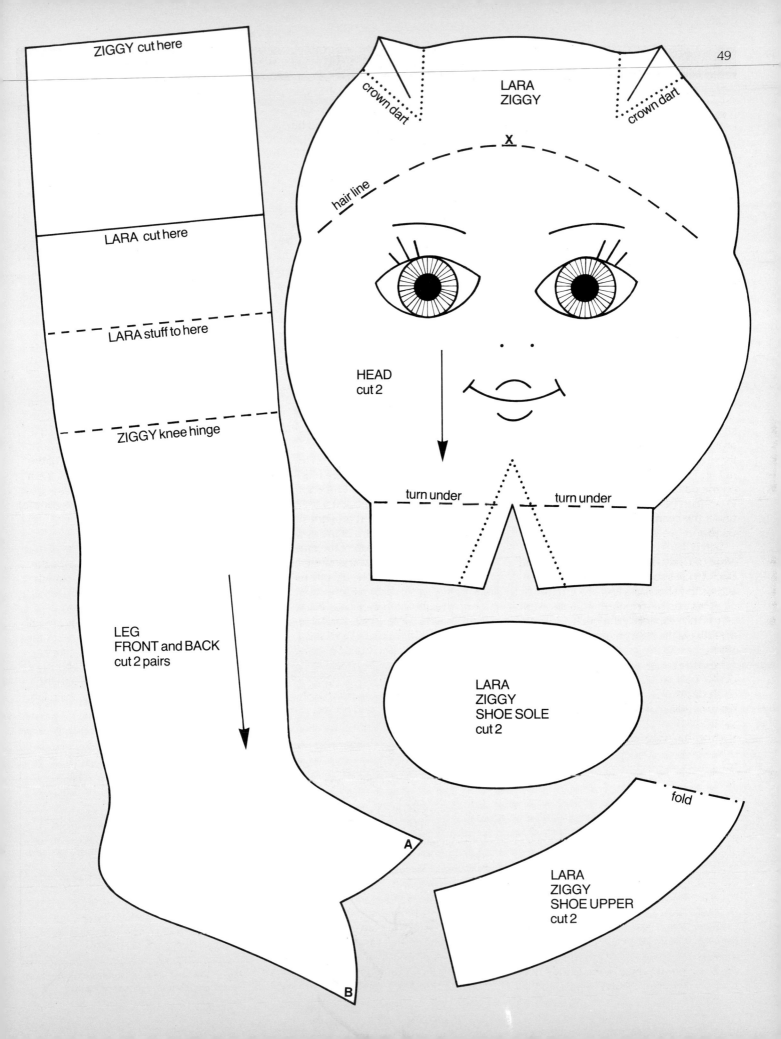

ZIGGY cut here

LARA cut here

LARA stuff to here

ZIGGY knee hinge

LEG
FRONT and BACK
cut 2 pairs

A

B

crown dart

LARA
ZIGGY

crown dart

X

hair line

HEAD
cut 2

turn under

turn under

LARA
ZIGGY
SHOE SOLE
cut 2

fold

LARA
ZIGGY
SHOE UPPER
cut 2

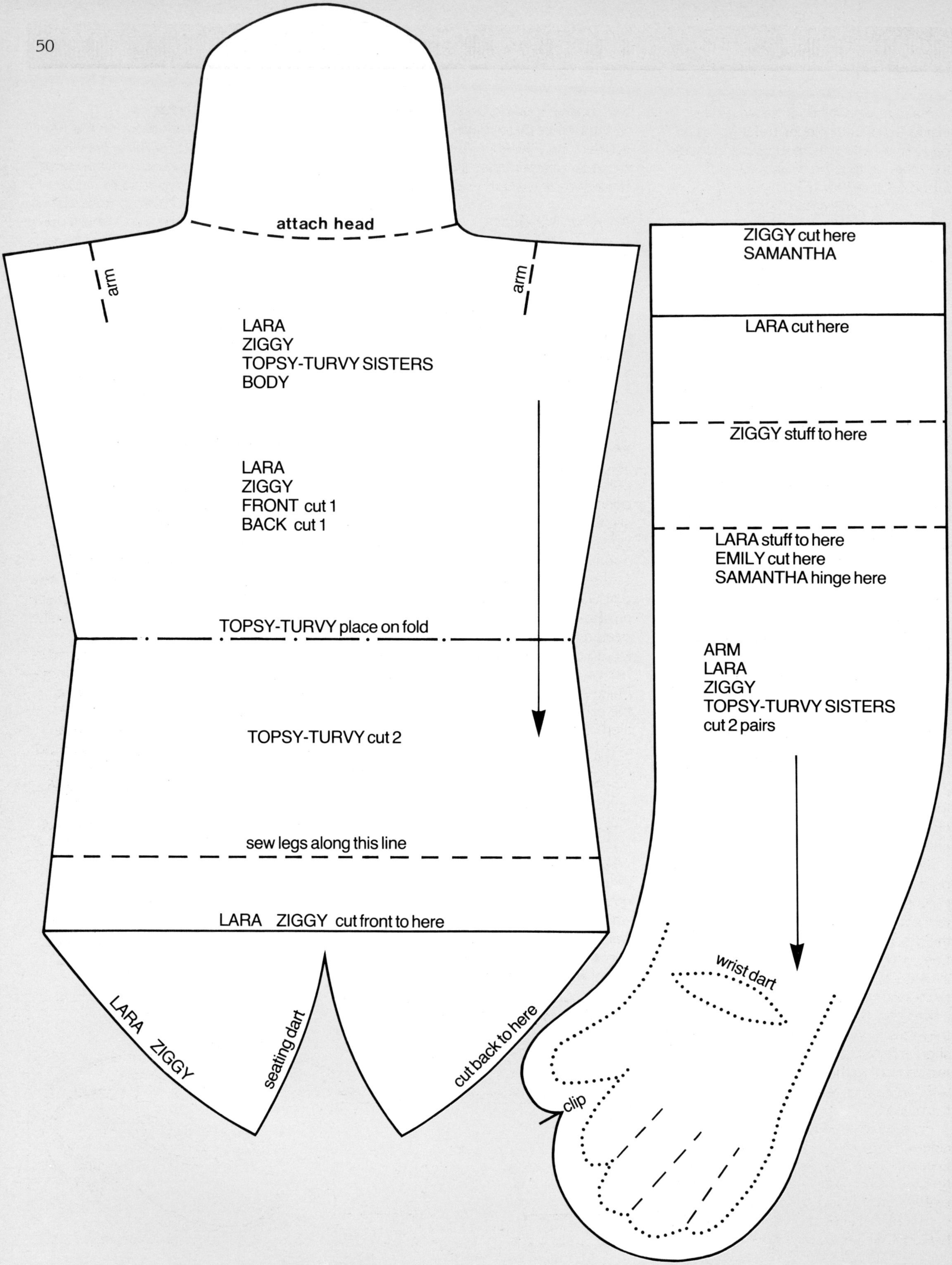

attach head

arm

arm

LARA
ZIGGY
TOPSY-TURVY SISTERS
BODY

LARA
ZIGGY
FRONT cut 1
BACK cut 1

TOPSY-TURVY place on fold

TOPSY-TURVY cut 2

sew legs along this line

LARA ZIGGY cut front to here

LARA ZIGGY

seating dart

cut back to here

ZIGGY cut here
SAMANTHA

LARA cut here

ZIGGY stuff to here

LARA stuff to here
EMILY cut here
SAMANTHA hinge here

ARM
LARA
ZIGGY
TOPSY-TURVY SISTERS
cut 2 pairs

wrist dart

clip

Make a narrow french seam on the inside leg of both pieces (refer to Fig 4, page 8) and then turn one section inside the other so that the wrong sides of fabric are together (Fig 3, page 48).

Machine-stitch a narrow centre front and back seam then turn through so that right sides of fabric are together and complete the french seam. Break the stitching where the seams cross to minimise the bulk.

Turn a deep double hem at the top edge and machine-stitch just below the edge and about 12mm (½in) beneath this, to form a channel for the elastic. Leave an opening in the channel at centre back. Thread the elastic through, pull it up to fit the Doll's waist and oversew the overlapped ends of plastic. Close the opening with hemming.

Petticoat

The petticoat has a lined bodice and a gathered skirt.

Work the Back and the Back lining and the Front and Front lining in the same way. Stitch the Back to the Front on the shoulder seams. Press open the seams. Pin and baste the bodice sections together with right sides facing and stitch the Back opening and neck edges together. Stitch round the armholes. Trim the seams and turn the bodice through to the right side, going carefully through the shoulders. Press the bodice. Open out the side seams of the bodice and lining and place them right sides together. Sew each side in one continuous seam. Press the seam flat and set the bodice aside.

Turn and press a narrow hem to the right side along the long edge of the petticoat skirt. Turn under and press the raw edge of the broderie anglaise. Lay the broderie anglaise over the folded hem covering the raw edge and stitch it in place. Fold and stitch two narrow tucks, approximately 12mm (½in) and 2.5cm (1in) above the hem line. Press the tucks towards the hem. Neaten both short sides of the Petticoat skirt. Work two rows of gathering stitches along the waist edge and gather up the waist to fit the bodice.

Pin the skirt and bodice together right sides facing, taking care to spread the fullness evenly. Machine-stitch and then trim the seam. Turn under the waist edge of the bodice lining and hem to the line of machine-stitching on the inside of the Petticoat. Sew two press fasteners on the

back opening of the Bodice after trying it on the Doll body to make sure the garment fits. The skirt remains open at the back, which makes it easier for children to dress and undress Lara.

Making the dress

The Dress Bodice is not lined. With wrong sides together stitch the Bodice Backs and the Front together on the shoulder and side seams. Turn and re-sew the seams making french seams. (Refer to Fig 4, page 8.) Press all seams towards the back. Make small tucks at the base of the frill line on the Front Bodice and baste in place on the waist edge.

Sleeve Join the Sleeve underarm with a french seam. Work a row of gathering stitches at the head of the Sleeve and pull it up until the Sleeve fits the armhole opening. With the Sleeve right side out slip the Sleeve into the Bodice, right sides facing and fit it into the armhole opening. Pin the underarm seam to the side seam of the bodice, distribute the gathers evenly then Backstitch the armhole seam. Oversew all raw edges to neaten the seam. Check the Sleeve length on the Doll, then fold a narrow hem at the wrist and slipstitch in place. Make and attach the second Sleeve in the same way.

Neck Edge Make a narrow double hem on both sides of the back opening of the Bodice. Apply the bias strip to the neck edge. Sew the trimming to the finished neck edge (see picture).

Frills Make the Bodice Frills by machine-stitching a narrow hem on both long edges of the Frill strips. Run a gathering thread along one edge and pull up the gathers until the Frill fits from the front waist edge, over the shoulder to the back waist edge. Baste and then sew the Frills in place. Cover the gathering line with trimming or narrow ribbon.

Finishing the Dress

Stitch the centre back seam on the Skirt to within 2.5cm (1in) of the waist edge. Work two rows of gathering at the waist edge and pull them up to fit the Bodice leaving 12mm (½in) over at each side of the opening. Stitch the skirt to the Bodice with right sides together. Trim the seam. Stitch a narrow double hem on the edges of the back opening, then neaten the seam edge of the skirt.

Fit the dress on the Doll to determine the length before turning up the bottom edge and hemming it. Cover the hem line with a row of trimming. Sew three press fasteners on the back opening at the neck, waist and in between.

Making the Shoes

Cut a narrow strip of felt for each Shoe. Fold it in half lengthways. Lay the fold against the inside edge of the Shoe and topstitch through all three layers of felt. This strengthens the Shoe on a potentially weak edge. Sew the heel edges of the Shoe together with a narrow seam. Insert the sole and baste it in place before sewing. Try the shoe on the Doll's foot to make sure that it fits before proceeding. Cut two strips of felt to make a Shoe strap (see picture). Top stitch the two layers together, shaping a point at one end. Cut a slit for the button and neaten the cut by working Buttonhole stitch all around it. Place the strap round the Doll's ankle to determine where the button should be sewn and then catch the strap to the back of the Shoe.

Make a second shoe in the same way but remember to turn the strap so that a pair of shoes is made.

Fig 4 *Fold the felt strip and stitch the front edge of the Shoe Upper along the strip to strengthen the edge of the Shoe*

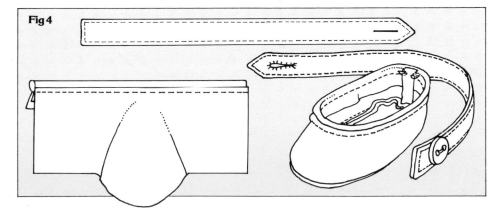

Fig 4

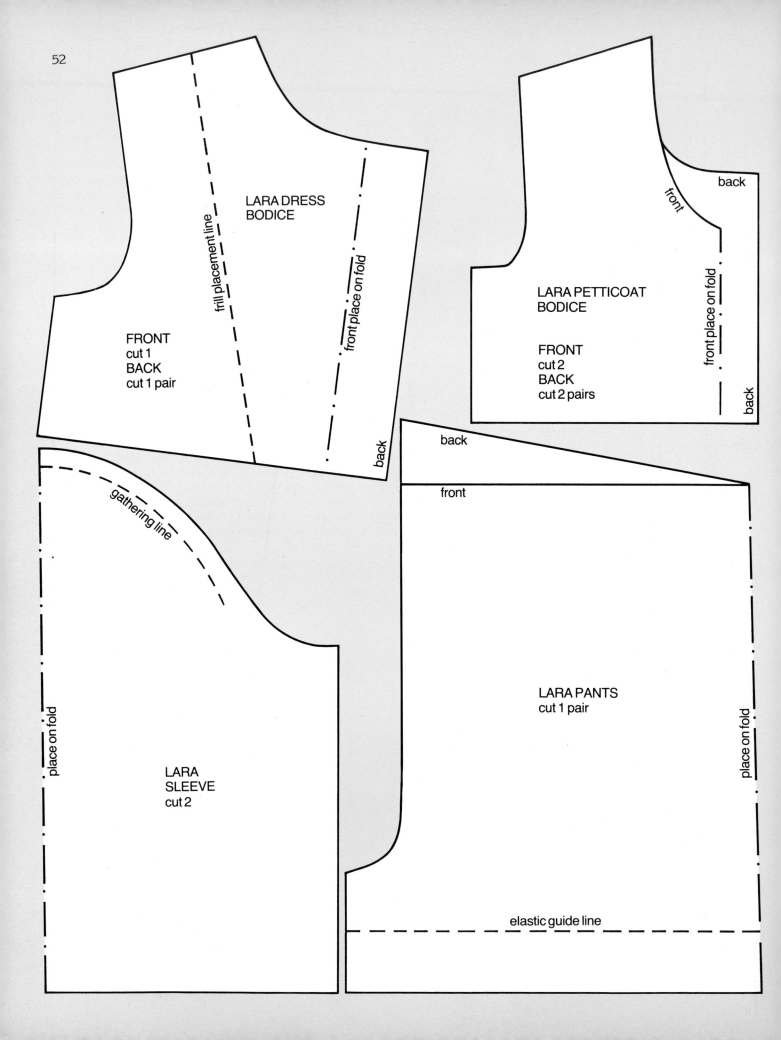

LARA DRESS
BODICE

frill placement line

front place on fold

FRONT
cut 1
BACK
cut 1 pair

back

LARA PETTICOAT
BODICE

FRONT
cut 2
BACK
cut 2 pairs

front

back

front place on fold

back

gathering line

place on fold

LARA
SLEEVE
cut 2

back

front

LARA PANTS
cut 1 pair

place on fold

elastic guide line

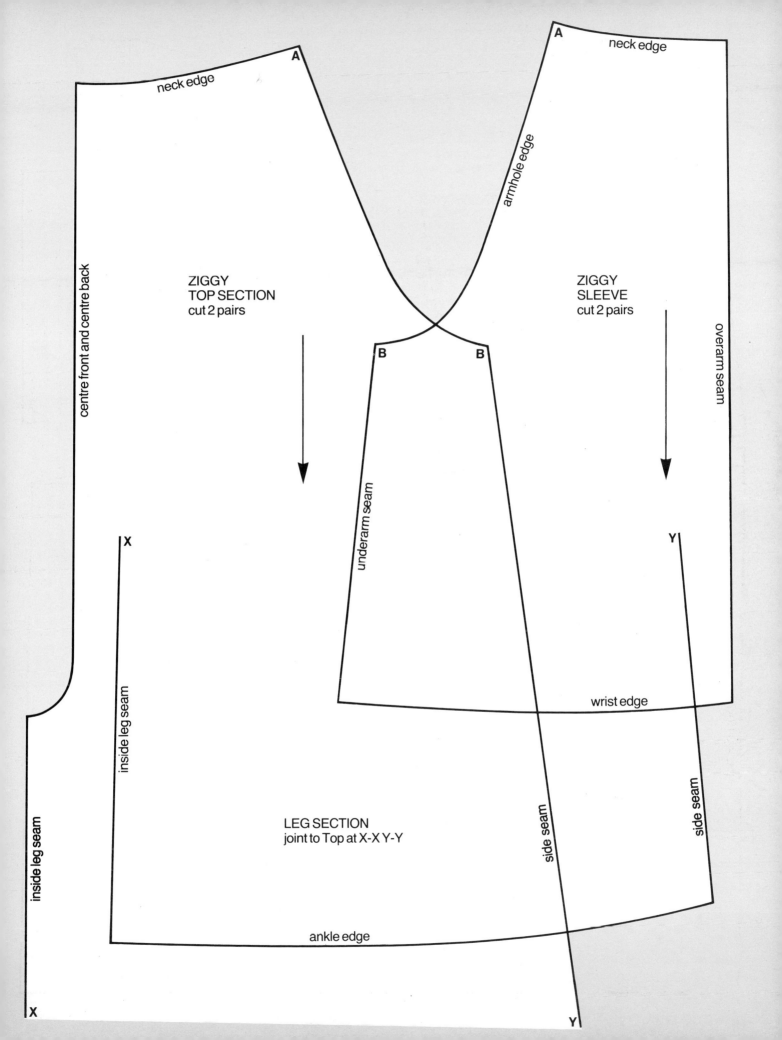

Ziggy

Ziggy the Clown and Lara share some of the pattern pieces on pages 49–50 with extra pattern pieces for Ziggy on page 52.

Materials required for Body

Finished size 46cm (18in) tall
46cm *(18in)* of 91cm *(36in)*-wide calico
170g *(6oz)* stuffing
25g *(1oz)* of yellow double knitting yarn
Stranded embroidery cotton, Black, Red and White
Red pencil (or lipstick)
Red, black and white felt, for facial features

Materials required for clothes

2 46cm *(18in)* squares of contrasting cotton
7cm *(2¾in)* by 112cm *(44in)*-wide piece of organza
23cm *(9in)* square of black felt
60cm *(24in)* of red bias binding

Making the pattern

Make card patterns of the Body, Head, Arm and Leg pieces from the trace-off patterns on pages 49 and 50 taking note of the special cutting lines for Ziggy. The Face detail is not required. Transfer all details.

Trace the garment patterns for Ziggy on page 52.

Because the body costume section is too large for the page, it has been cut into two sections to fit the page. First trace the top section of the costume to X–Y, then reposition the tracing on the lower leg section matching X–X and Y–Y and continue tracing to the ankle edge. The half sleeve pattern is superimposed

on the body section so take care to follow the correct outline when tracing. Make a card pattern or use the tracings to cut out fabrics. A 6mm *(¼in)* seam allowance is given on all pieces.

Cutting out

Cut a Body, Arms and Legs from calico. The costume is made from two fabrics. Lay the squares of fabric on the table with the wrong sides together. For the Front cut a pair each of half Sleeve and Body sections, checking that one half of each uses one fabric while the second half uses the contrasting fabric. Cut the Back exactly the same as the Front.

Cut the Shoes and the two edging strips from black felt.

Circles of felt are needed for the facial features. Smear clear adhesive on the back of the felt piece. Leave it to dry before cutting out the features. Cut a 5cm *(2in)*-diameter red felt circle for the nose. Cut two 2cm *(¾in)*-diameter white felt circles for the eye backing and two 12mm *(½in)*-diameter black felt circles for the pupils.

Making the Doll

Make the Arms as directed for Lara. Turn them right side out and stuff the hands gently, with just a small amount of filling. Topstitch the fingers with button thread. Anchor the end of the thread by Backstitching inconspicuously along the Arm seam, then bring the thread out at the base of one of the fingers and Stab-stitch to the top of the fingers, pulling on each stitch to sink it in the fabric. Work all the finger divisions in the same way, then finish off by Backstitching along the Arm seam. Finish the Arms as for Lara.
Legs Make the Legs as for Lara, and stuff to the line just above knee level (see pattern). Hold the stuffing in place with a pin or needle. Work a row of small running stitches across the knee with button thread to enable the Legs to bend. Stuff the upper section of the Legs lightly and finish them as described for Lara's legs.

Complete the Doll by making the Head and Body, then attaching the Arms and legs. Refer back to the instructions for making Lara if necessary.

Working the features

Run a gathering thread around the nose felt circle and pull it up, filling the cavity with stuffing. Pull the gathering up to

make a firm ball. Fasten off the thread ends then Ladder-stitch in place on the face. For the mouth, anchor six strands of red embroidery thread in the eye position, then bring the needle out on the cheek below the eye and make a long loop over to the cheek on the other side. Hold the loop down in a curve with two tiny straight stitches (Fig 1) and fasten off the thread in the other eye position.

Smear lipstick on the ball of the little finger and gently rub the cheeks with a circular motion to colour them.

Stab-stitch the black pupils to the eye whites with two strands of black thread in the needle. Embroider the eye highlights with a few white stitches at 1 o'clock (see picture). Fasten all six strands of black embroidery thread on the face in the eye position. Place a small spot of glue behind the eye and position it on the face. (The glue will hold the eye steady.) Work two long Straight stitches in black completely over the eye and hold them together in the centre of the eye with a small straight stitch. Fasten off the thread by backstitching invisibly around the eye between layers of black and white felt. Work the second eye in the same way.

Hair

Cut a piece of card 15 × 6.5cm *(6 × 2½in)*. Wind knitting yarn round the card. Cut along one edge of the card to release the yarn, then feed the short lengths under the machine foot and stitch a central seam (see Fig 2). Continue in this way until all the wool is used up. All the strips of wool sewn together should make a length of approximately 75cm *(30in)*. Backstitch the strip to the Head along the stitched seam. Frame the face

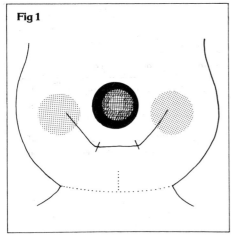

Fig 1 *Embroidery for Ziggy's mouth: hold the looped thread down with straight stitches*

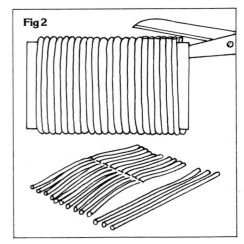

Fig 2 *Making hair for Ziggy: wind yarn round the card. Cut and stitch along the loops on the top edge*

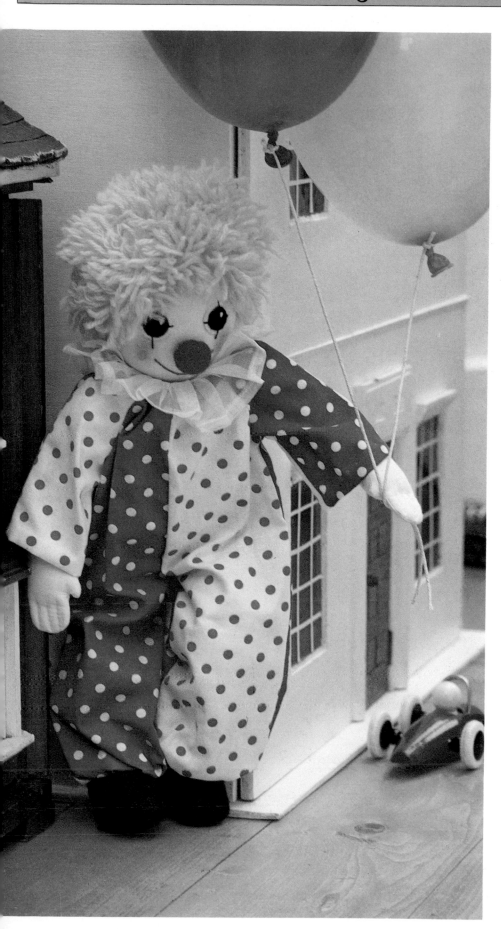

first, then work spirally around the Head, finishing on the crown. Trim uneven ends neatly to finish.

Making the clothes

Take each pair of Body sections and stitch them together down the centre front and centre back seams respectively. Similarly, stitch each pair of half Sleeves together down the arm seam. With fabrics alternating, stitch a Sleeve to the Body along the armhole edge A–B on both front and back edges. Stitch the other Sleeve in place. Stitch the arm and side seams, breaking the stitching at B. Stitch the inside leg seam down to the ankle edge on each side in turn.

Turn under a narrow double hem on the wrist edges. Fit the costume on the Doll by feeding the feet down through the ankle edges (the costume is inside out at this stage). Run a gathering thread along the ankle edges and pull up so that they fit tightly against the legs.

Backstitch the Trousers in place through the gathers, attaching them to the legs making sure that the side seams of the costume and the inside leg seams are not twisted out of place. Finish both ankle edges in the same way.

Pull the costume onto the Body, inserting the arms in the Sleeves. Turn under the neck edge and gather it up to fit the body; fasten off the thread ends.

Making the neck frill

Make a narrow double hem along both short edges and one long edge of the organza strip. Gather the raw long edge and pull it up to fit Ziggy's neck. Match the centre of the bias binding to the centre of the right side of the frill. Stitch it in place and trim the seam. Fold the bias binding over to the wrong side of the frill and hem it in place, then machine-stitch through the edge of the bias to hold the fold in place along the entire length. Knot both ends of the bias binding and trim the ends. Place the frill round the neckline and tie it in place. The ties can hang down in front to add more colour, or be finished with a bow. Finish dressing Ziggy by making the felt shoes as described for Lara but omitting the straps.

Sew the bottoms of the trousers to the shoes to hold them on the feet.

Make woolly pompoms to decorate the costume and shoes if desired.

Patterns for Ziggy are on pages 49–50 and 52

The Topsy-Turvy Sisters

Topsy-Turvy or Upside-Down dolls are a popular novelty. Over the years they have developed from ethnic dolls, to 'awake and asleep' dolls, then to storybook characters.

The Topsy-Turvy Sisters doll is a variation of the 'awake and asleep' doll and is an interesting exercise in working the same pattern in different fabrics. Baby Emily has a needle-sculptured stretch stockinette head and arms, while Sister Samantha has head and arms made of calico. The Sisters share a common body, joined at the waist.

Materials required for Baby Emily
Finished size 48cm (19in) tall
23cm (9in) of 91cm (36in)-wide flesh-coloured stockinette
23cm (9in) square of muslin
23cm (9in) of non-woven interfacing, either iron-on medium stretch or iron-on soft
227g (8oz) of stuffing
Small ball of flaxen-coloured knitting yarn
One 3¾mm (No. 9) knitting needle

Lipstick for cheek colouring
Stranded embroidery cotton
Flesh-coloured sewing thread
1m (1yd) of white cotton lawn
Ribbons
Broderie anglaise

Materials required for Samantha
46cm (½yd) of calico
Small piece of black felt
Lipstick for cheek colouring
Stranded embroidery cotton, Pink
25g (1oz) of double knitting yarn
Narrow ribbon
60cm (24in) of patterned fabric
Lace trimming
Clear adhesive

Making the pattern
Using the Body pattern for Lara, place a piece of folded tracing paper against the fold line marked on the pattern. Draw around the top half of the Body and neck, then cut out. Open out the folded paper to reveal two similar upper bodies which are joined at the waist. Make a card pattern.

Use the Arm pattern for Ziggy to make Samantha's Arm. Make a card pattern of the same Arm for Emily but cut it off at Lara's stuffing line. Mark all the relevant details, including the wrist dart for

Samantha, which will reduce the thickness in the lower arm. Make a card pattern of the three Head pieces (page 59) which are used for both Sisters.

The Skirt, Bodice and Sleeve measurements are the same for both dolls and are as follows:
Skirt: 38cm (15in) by 91cm (36in) wide
Bodice: 13cm (5in) by 27cm (10½in) wide
Sleeve: 18cm (7in) by 20cm (8in) wide
In addition, Emily has a two-piece bonnet. The brim measures 10.5cm (4½in) by 27cm (10½in) wide, while the crown is a 5cm (2in) circle. The frill at the bottom of Emily's gown is made from two strips, each measuring 91cm (36in) by 5cm (2in).

Cutting out
Cut Samantha's Head, Arms and Body from calico. Cut her Dress Skirt, Bodice and two Sleeves from the patterned fabric. A 6mm (¼in) seam allowance and generous hem allowance is included on all pieces.

Spread clear adhesive on the back of the felt. When dry, cut two 1cm (⅜in)-diameter black felt circles for the eye pupils, and one 2cm (¾in)-diameter circle for the nose from stockinette.

For Emily, draw all three Head pieces onto non-woven interfacing and iron these to the stockinette before cutting out, making sure to cut a pair of Side Heads.

Fold the remaining stockinette and place the muslin beneath it. Pin at the corners to hold the fabrics together. Draw the outline of the Arms on the top layer of stockinette, then stitch through all three layers 6mm (¼in) inside the cutting line, leaving the top straight edge open. Cut out the Arms.

Cut Skirt, Skirt Frills, Bodice, two Sleeves, Bonnet Brim and two crown circles from the white fabric, following the measurements given.

Making the dolls
Start by stitching the Front and Back Body sections together round the edges. Make a 5cm (2in) slash on one side of the Body, across the waist. Turn the Body right side out through the slash, stuff very firmly then close with Ladder stitch. The slash should lie on the back of the Doll.

Sew the calico Head sections together to make Samantha's head. Stitch the neck darts on the Head Front and both Side Heads, then stitch the front to the side B–A on each side in turn. Stitch the back to the sides C–D on each side in turn. Trim the seams, turn the Head right side out and stuff firmly. Make sure that the cheeks are even.

Turn the neck edge under evenly and baste it. Push a thumb up into the head until a socket has been made large enough to fit the body neck stalk. Ladder-stitch the Head in place and remove the basting. Push the stuffing down from the crown of the Head to finish shaping it then Ladder-stitch between A–C.

Make Emily's Head in the same way but take care not to overstuff it as this will distort the shape. Stitch the Head onto the other end of the Body, first checking that both Sisters are facing in the same direction.

Skirts Seam the short ends of each Skirt piece together. With right sides together and raw edges level, stitch them together along one edge, which will be the hem edge of the dresses. The short seams should lie centre back.

Join the Skirt frills together on short ends to make a long strip. Neaten the long edges and trim one with broderie anglaise. Gather the other edge and pull it up to fit the skirt. Stitch the frill in place, the lower edge level with the join of both skirts. The frill will just show through to form a petticoat edging for Samantha (page 58, Fig 2).

Gather the waist edge of the patterned skirt and pull it up to fit the Doll. Stitch it in place by Backstitching it around the waist. Turn the Doll upside-down and gather Emily's Skirt to fit the Body, Backstitching it in place as before. The centre back seams of the Skirts will be on opposite sides to the Dolls' faces.

Bodices Fold under the long edge of Samantha's Bodice and slipstitch it over the gathered Skirt waist. Overlap the short edges at the back, turn under a single hem and continue slipstitching up to the neck edge. Turn under the top edge of the Bodice to fit the Doll, fold the corners on to the shoulders and sew in place. Decorate the Bodice with lace gathered to fit from the waist, around the neck and back to the waist at the centre front.

Make Emily's Bodice in the same way and decorate down the centre front with broderie anglaise trimming, finishing with a long bow sewn in place. Emily also has a gathered broderie anglaise neck frill.

Arms and Sleeves

To make Samantha's Arms, stitch the wrist dart on a pair of calico Arm pieces. These will become the inside arms, as there is no dart on the outer arm pieces. Then stitch the Arms together in pairs, trim the seams, clip the thumbs and turn right side out. Stuff the Arms and top-stitch the fingers as described for Ziggy. Turn in the top edge, making small pleats on each side and close the opening.

Turn a 2cm (¾in) hem along one long edge of the sleeve piece. Stitch lace to this folded edge, then stitch the short sides together. Run a gathering thread around the wrist, about 12mm (½in) back from the edge. Push the Arm down through the Sleeve, pull up the gathers to fit and stitch in place around the wrist. Finish the Sleeve by turning in the top and stitching it as for the top of the Arm, but do not catch the Arm to the Sleeve. Sew the Sleeve to the top of the Shoulder. The Arm should move quite freely. Finish the other Arm in the same way, and sew it to the Body.

Emily's Arms must be made carefully, or they will look chunky and distorted. Stitch the Arms in pairs as described but

omit the wrist darts. Turn them right side out and lightly stuff the hands.

Hands Topstitch the fingers, starting at the base of each finger and working towards the top. Finish each finger by taking the thread over the top and back into the finger underneath and pulling up the thread to shape the fingers. There is no stitching between fingers and thumb. A small line of single stitching can be added at the base of, but separate from, the finger stitching to indicate dimples.

Insert stuffing into the palm of the hand, then stitch the wrist by working a row of very small running stitches all around it and pulling up the thread before fastening off on the seam line.

Stuff the Arm lightly, then bend it at the elbow (page 58, Fig 1). Stroke the crease evenly with the needle, then Ladder-stitch the folds together on each side of the crease. This effectively works a dart on the surface. Close the top of the Arm, folding in the sides. Make the second Arm in the same way.

Make the Sleeves as described for Samantha, but note that there will be a more generous turn-in at the top, and that the Arms are tilted to whatever position required. Make a small catch

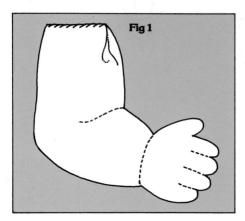

Fig 1 *The Arm showing top-stitched fingers, wrist shaping and elbow crease*

stitch between the inside Sleeve and Arm to hold the Arm at the chosen angle. Sew the completed Arms to the shoulders after checking the length.

Samantha's hair and face

Samantha's face has felt pupils and embroidered detail. Work a few straight stitches in white thread at 11 o'clock for the highlights, then sew the pupils in place and embroider the eyelids and lashes as indicated on the pattern on page 59. Blush the cheeks with lipstick and embroider a mouth in Stem Stitch.
Hair For the hair cut 111 strands of wool, each 30cm *(12in)* long. Divide them into three equal bunches of 37 strands. Take one bunch at a time, spread the wool evenly then machine-stitch the strands together 9cm *(3½in)* from each end (Fig 3). Lay the first bunch across the top back of the Head and sew it to the Head on each side through the stitching, on the line marked 1 on pattern. Lay the second bunch lower on the back of the Head and sew it down on each side on the line marked 2 which crosses over 1. The last bunch lies over the crown and is stitched horizontally over previous bunches. Make sure that all bunches are pulled taut as stitches are worked. Backstitch a central parting from the forehead to the back of the Head. In this way the hair will be securely fastened. Cover the stitching at the ears with two ribbon bows. Trim the hair bunches to the required length.

Emily's features

Emily's face is framed with a few rows of curls, while the rest of the head is covered by her bonnet. The curls are made by winding yarn over a knitting needle from the pointed end towards the

Fig 2 *The Skirt showing the shared hem edge and the frilled edge of Emily's Dress*

top (from left to right along the needle). Load the needle with several windings of yarn, then Stem-stitch the curls together with double sewing thread in a matching colour. Push most of the curls off the needle, then continue winding on more wool and stitching until about 1m *(1⅛yd)* of curls has been made. Backstitch the curls round the front of the face.
Eyes and Nose Embroider the eyes as shown on the pattern (page 59), using two strands of stranded cotton. Finish the eyes by transferring the thread to a long needle and taking it through to the back of the Head from each corner of

Fig 3

Fig 3 *Making Samantha's hair: bunch the 30cm (12in)-long strands by stitching 9cm (3½in) from the ends. Position the bunch on the Doll*

the eyes in turn. Pull up the thread and fasten off to sink the eyes into sockets.

In the same way, take a few stitches through the Head from the nose position to the back and pull it up before fastening off. Run a gathering thread around the nose circle and insert a tiny piece of stuffing before pulling it up to form a small ball nose. Fasten off the thread ends. Trim the stalk of the nose short, then Ladder-stitch it to the face with the remainder of the nose stalk sitting in the 'nose socket'. Blush the cheeks with lipstick.

If necessary, take a few stitches through the Head from side to side where the ears would be, pull up the thread to emphasise the cheeks, then fasten off the thread ends. Needle-modelling faces is an acquired skill and it takes some time to get them just right. Practise on a spare surface first, to get the tension of the stitches perfect.
Bonnet To make the Bonnet. Hem both short sides and one long edge of the brim piece. Trim the front edge with wide double-edged trimming threaded with ribbon to match the bodice front. Gather the remaining long edge. Place the two crown circles together with right sides facing and stitch around the edge. Make a small slash on one side and turn right side out. Slipstitch in place to cover the gathered edge of the brim. Finally, sew ribbons to the edge of the bonnet and tie in a bow under the Doll's chin.

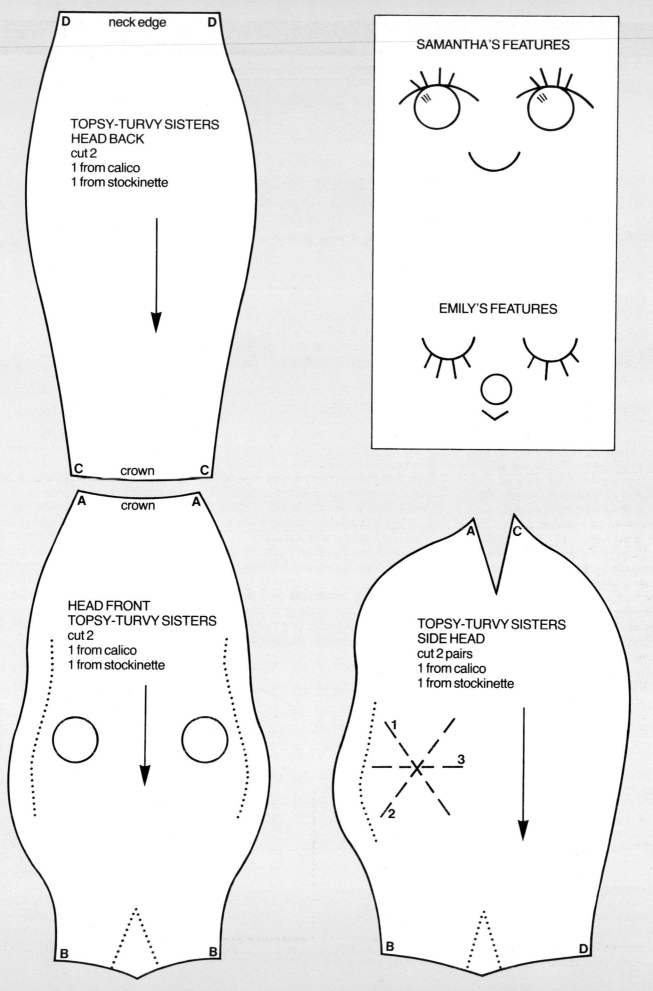

D neck edge **D**

TOPSY-TURVY SISTERS
HEAD BACK
cut 2
1 from calico
1 from stockinette

C crown **C**

A crown **A**

HEAD FRONT
TOPSY-TURVY SISTERS
cut 2
1 from calico
1 from stockinette

B **B**

SAMANTHA'S FEATURES

EMILY'S FEATURES

A **C**

TOPSY-TURVY SISTERS
SIDE HEAD
cut 2 pairs
1 from calico
1 from stockinette

1
3
2

B **D**

Patchwork Toys

Circles of gaily-coloured cotton fabrics, gathered to make Suffolk puffs, is a traditional patchwork technique and one which is also popular with toymakers. When threaded onto elastic, puffs make stretchy animals and dolls. Although the circles can be random-coloured for some toys, a more balanced scheme is needed for the alligator and mice. Try grouping similar colours together for sections of the alligator's body, remembering the value of a plain green to separate busy patterns.

Alligator

Older children could help to make the Suffolk Puffs for the Alligator – only Running stitches are required to form them.

Materials required

Finished size approximately 41cm (16in) long
18cm *(7in)* square of green velvet or very short pile fur
23cm *(9in)* square of green felt
1 pair of 16mm *(⅝in)* white and green safety eyes with moving pupils
Small amount of stuffing
13cm *(5in)* of narrow white ric-rac braid
61cm *(24in)* of narrow elastic
Assorted pieces of patterned and plain green fabrics
Embroidery cotton, white

Making the pattern

From the trace-off half-pattern on page 62, trace the Alligator's Head on folded tracing paper and re-trace to make the complete pattern. Trace the Foot. Prepare card patterns. Transfer all marks and details.

Draw and cut out a set of card circles to the following diameter measurements. Mark each with an identifying letter.

A: 7.5cm   *(3in)*
B: 9cm   *(3½in)*
C: 10cm   *(4in)*
D: 11.5cm *(4½in)*
E: 12.5cm *(5in)*
F: 14cm   *(5½in)*
G: 15cm   *(6in)*

Cutting out

Cut a Head from the velvet or fur. Cut the piece of felt in half and on one half draw around the Foot outline four times, each foot separated from the next by at least 6mm *(¼in)*. Lay the second piece of felt

under the first, then pin both layers together through the centre of each Foot.

Place the card circles on fabric and draw round them using the same fabric for each circle size. Pin three or four layers of fabric together so that several circles can be cut out together. You will require the following: A: 44 circles B: 7 circles C: 6 circles D: 8 circles E: 8 circles F: 3 circles G: 10 circles.

Cut out the circles and put each set into a separate plastic bag. Label the bags with the identifying letter.

Making Suffolk Puffs

Fold all the fabric circles (except one A circle) into quarters and snip off the point to make a small hole (Fig 1a). Finger-press a narrow hem around the edge of the circle, then run a double gathering thread round the hem (Fig 1b). Pull up the gathers, drawing the edges inwards to meet, then fasten off the thread ends. Flatten the circle into a Puff (Fig 1c). Lay aside 5 A Puffs without gathering them. These are for the Tail.

Replace the Puffs in the plastic bags so that they can be identified.

Making the Alligator's Head

Stitch darts on each side of the Head. Fold the Head right sides facing and stitch the seam A–B. Turn the head right side out. Insert the eyes with the domed side uppermost. (Refer to Fig 1 page 12 for the technique.)

Stuff the Head firmly to within 18mm *(¾in)* of the opening. Fold the sides of the opening to the middle and catch the edges together with a stitch (Fig 2a). Fold up the bottom edge of the opening and oversew the edge over the holding stitch (Fig 2b).

Cut the elastic in half. On one piece, fold a loop at one end and sew across to hold the loop (Fig 3a). Press the loop flat

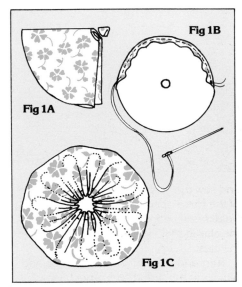

Fig 1A   *Fold the circle of fabric twice then cut off the corner to make a central hole*

Fig 1B   *Turn a narrow single hem on the circles, gather the fabric into a Puff*

Fig 1C   *Pull up the thread to form the Puff. The Puff is smoother on the reverse side*

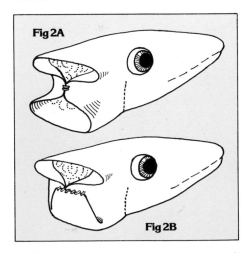

Fig 2A   *Bring the opening sides to the middle and catch together with stitches*

Fig 2B   *Fold the bottom edge of the opening over the edge, then oversew over the stitches*

and sew the elastic to the oversewn edge of the Head opening (Fig 3b and 3c). Fold the top edge of the Head down over the elastic and oversew the edge to cover the elastic loop.

Turn under the ends of the ric-rac and pin along the mouth placement lines. Sew in place with small white straight stitches that go over each point of ric-rac, to resemble sharp teeth (see picture).

Making the Feet

Machine-stitch on the marked outline of each Foot piece, stitching through both layers of felt. Cut out the Feet close to the stitching. Cut a small central slit in the top layer of each Foot and turn right side out.

Stuff the feet and leave the slit open. Cut the remaining elastic in half and sew a small loop on one end of both pieces (as Fig 3a). Set aside one piece of elastic.

Push the elastic loop through the slit into a Foot, then oversew the slit to close it, securing the elastic at the same time (Fig 4a). Thread 7 A Puffs onto the elastic from the smooth side of the Puffs

then 7 more A Puffs, but this time thread through the gathered side. Pull up the elastic tightly, trim away any excess elastic and sew a loop on the free end (Fig 4b). Insert the loop in the Foot and secure with sewing as before. Catch down the puff nearest to each foot to hide the oversewn slits. This makes a pair of legs with 7 small puffs for each leg. Complete another pair of legs on the second piece of elastic in the same way. Set all four legs aside until the body is completed.

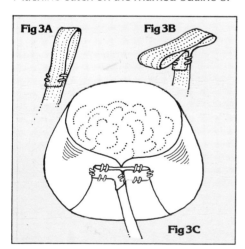

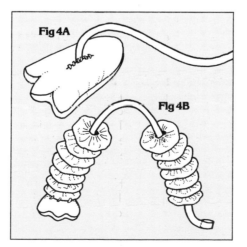

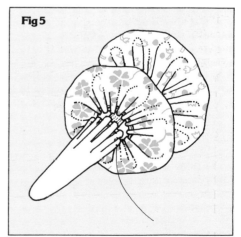

Fig 3A   Fold the elastic end into a loop and sew

Fig 3B   Flatten the loop ready to sew to the Head opening

Fig 3C   Sew the loop to the Head opening

Fig 4A   Slip the elastic loop into the stuffed Foot, oversew the slit to close and secure with stitches

Fig 4B   Thread 7 Puffs on the elastic from the smooth side, then 7 more to make the second leg

Fig 5   Cover the elastic end with the last Puff, pushing it up against the previous Puff. Ladder-stitch the two Puffs together to further secure the elastic

Assembling the Alligator

The Body is assembled by threading Puffs onto the elasic attached to the Head. Begin by threading 2 D Puffs from the smooth side with the gathered side of Puffs towards the tail. Continue threading Puffs as follows: 3E, 10G, 3F, 5E, 6D, 6C, 7B, 10A.

On the 5 unfinished A Puffs, turn a deeper hem and gather the edges (Fig 1) to make smaller Puffs. Thread these on the elastic. Pull up the elastic and cut off any excess. Sew a loop on the end (Fig 3). Slip a pencil through the loop to hold the elastic. To make the remaining Puff, gather the edges without snipping a hole. Enclose the elastic loop inside the Puff

and then finish off the thread ends taking stitches through the elastic. Catch the last two Puffs together to further secure the elastic (Fig 5).

Attaching the Legs

The first pair of Legs is attached to the body between the sixth and seventh puffs behind the Head and the second pair of Legs is attached between the twenty-second and twenty-third puffs. Push the Puffs apart and loop the legs over the body elastic. Make sure that each Leg has 7 Puffs. Sew the edges of the Legs elastic together so that the Body elastic is free to move within the loop. Secure both pairs of Legs in the same way.

The Mice

When making these Suffolk Puff toys remember that the weight of the fabric used may determine the length of arms and legs. Be prepared to adjust the number of Puffs accordingly.

Materials required for both mice

Finished size approximately 23cm (9in) tall

23cm (9in) square of short pile white fur
23cm (9in) square of pink felt
15cm (6in) square of felt for shoes
2 pairs 9mm (⅜in) amber safety eyes
Stranded embroidery cotton for nose
Small amount of stuffing
1.5m (1⅝yd) of narrow elastic
46cm (18in) of narrow broderie anglaise
50cm (20in) piece of 91cm (31in)-wide white cotton fabric
Approximately 50cm (20in) of mixed cotton fabrics for the Girl Mouse Dress
30cm (12in) of fine check fabric for shirt
Approximately 50cm (20in) of mixed cotton fabrics for Boy Mouse Trousers

Making the pattern

Trace the Mice patterns from the trace-off pattern on page 64 and prepare card patterns. Transfer all marks and details. The Head and Body have a 6mm (¼in) seam allowance included. Draw and cut out a set of card circles to the following diameter measurements:
Mark each circle with an identifying letter.
A: 7.5cm   (3in)
B: 9cm   (3½in)
C: 10cm   (4in)
D: 12.5cm   (5in)

Cutting out

For the Boy Mouse, cut a pair of Heads from white fur and a pair of Bodies from the checked fabric. For the Girl Mouse, cut a pair of white fur Heads and a pair of Bodies from patterned Dress fabric.

For the Boy Mouse Puffs, cut fabric circles as follows: B: 20 from Shirt fabric, E: 6, C: 2 and B: 30 from Trousers fabrics.

For the Girl Mouse, cut fabric circles as follows: B: 24 from Dress fabrics, C: 4 and A: 34 from white cotton fabric.

Cut a Petticoat from white cotton fabric 15 × 40cm (6 × 16in). Cut Skirt from patterned Dress fabric 16 × 60cm (6½ × 24in).

Cut out two felt Ears for each Mouse. Draw out two fur Ears but do not cut them out at this stage. Cut the remaining

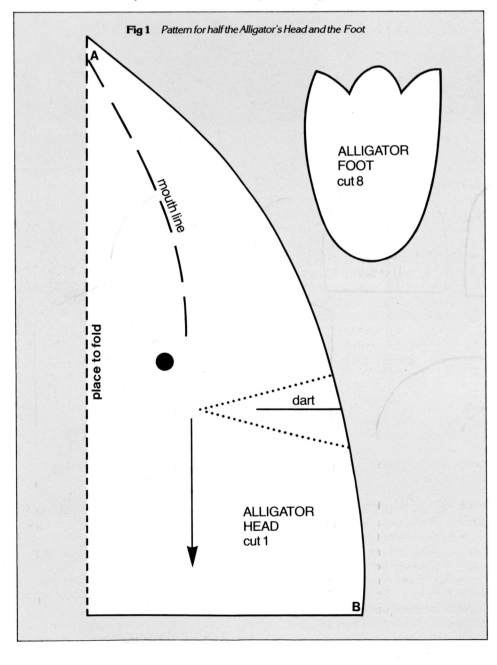

Fig 1   Pattern for half the Alligator's Head and the Foot

A

place to fold

mouth line

dart

ALLIGATOR FOOT
cut 8

ALLIGATOR HEAD
cut 1

B

pink felt in half and on one piece draw around the Hands four times for each Mouse. (The remaining felt may be used for a tail for the Boy Mouse if desired.) Place the second piece of pink felt underneath, then machine-stitch the Hands just inside the marked outline leaving the straight edge open. Cut out and turn the Hands right side out. Cut the Shoe felt in half. For each Mouse, draw the outline of the Shoe four times on one piece, lay the second piece underneath and machine-stitch round the outline,

just inside the marked line. Cut out on the marked line.

Making the Boy Mouse

Stitch the Body pieces together right sides facing, leaving the waist edge open. Turn the skin right side out and stuff firmly. Turn under the raw edges and gather up the opening, pulling the edges inwards. Fasten off the thread ends.

Stitch the Head pieces together right sides facing leaving the straight neck edge open. Turn right side out.

Insert the safety eyes (refer to Fig 1, page 12) and stuff the Head firmly. Run a gathering thread around the neck and pull it up until the head fits over the neck projection of the body. Ladder-stitch the Head to the Body.

Ears Make a pair of Ears by laying the felt Ear pieces on the wrong side of the marked fur Ears. Topstitch round the curved edge, taking in a very small seam allowance. Cut out the Ears being very careful to follow the felt outline and cutting only the fur backing, not the pile.

Tease the trapped pile from the seam by gently 'stroking' the fur with a needle. Ladder-stitch the ears to the Head where indicated.

Nose and Whiskers Work a few Satin stitches for the nose. Whiskers are optional and will depend very much on the age of the future owner – older children prefer more realism.

Suffolk Puffs Arms

Make the 20 B Puffs following the instructions on page 60, Figs 1a, 1b and 1c.

Cut two pieces of elastic, each 18cm (7in) long. Fold over the end of the elastic and stitch a loop approximately 4cm (¾in) from the end. Press the loops flat then sew them securely to the sides of the Body at the shoulder. Make and attach the second piece of elastic to the shoulder on the other side. Thread 10 Puffs on each Arm elastic with the gathered side lying towards the Hands.

Sew the first Puff on each Arm to the Body at the shoulder so that it hides the elastic. Pull the Arm elastic so that the Puffs are pushed closely together. Trim away the excess elastic. Stitch a small loop at the end. Put a pencil in the loop to hold the elastic in place.

Stuff the felt Hands then remove the pencil and carefully insert the loop into the Hand and sew the elastic into the opening, drawing the edges together round the elastic. Sew the last Puff to the Hand. Finish the Arm on the other side in the same way.

Making the Trousers and Pants

Fold a 38cm (15in) length of elastic in half. Stitch the fold securely to the waist gathers on the Body. Make all the Pants and Trouser Puffs and thread the 6 largest Puffs onto the doubled elastic. Separate for the Leg elastics and, on each Leg, thread first a C Puff and then 15 B puffs. Pull up the elastic and sew loops on the ends as for the Arms.

Shoes Make a small central slit through the top of each Shoe, turn right side out and then stuff the Shoes. Insert the Leg loops and sew to secure the loop and close the slit. Cover the slit by sewing an ankle Puff to the Shoe. Finish both Legs in the same way. Sew the felt tail to the back of the Mouse between the large Trouser puffs. Fasten a short length of ribbon around the neck and tie it in place.

Making the Girl Mouse

The Girl Mouse is made in the same way as the Boy Mouse except that she has 12 Puffs to each sleeve instead of 10. The Pants start with 4 Puffs, then each Leg has 17 smaller puffs.

Join the short ends of the Petticoat piece with a narrow french seam. Hem the lower edge and trim with broderie anglaise trimming.

Turn a hem on the waist edge and gather it. Pull up the Petticoat waist to fit between the Body waist and the first Puff of the Pants.

Join the short ends of the Skirt piece and neaten the seams. Hand-sew a hem along the bottom edge. Measure down from the waist to determine the length required, then turn and stitch a hem at the waist edge. Gather the waist and sew it to the Body through the gathers.

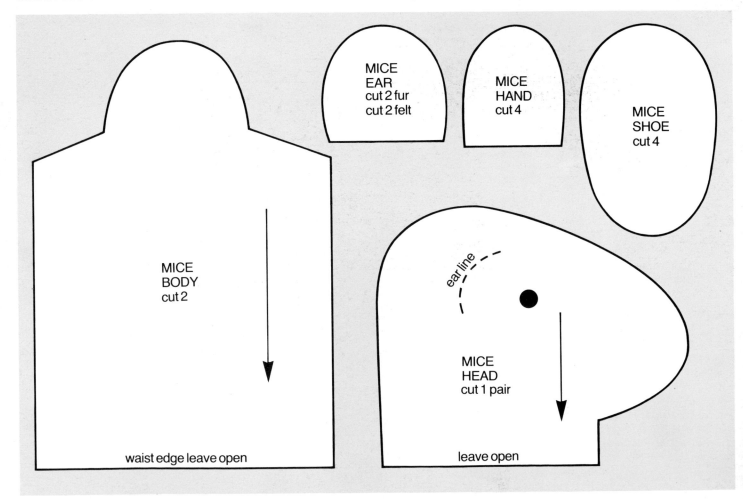

MICE EAR cut 2 fur cut 2 felt

MICE HAND cut 4

MICE SHOE cut 4

MICE BODY cut 2

MICE HEAD cut 1 pair

ear line

waist edge leave open

leave open